His "Incalculable"
Influence on Others:
Essays on Robert Frost
in Our Time

edited by EARL J. WILCOX

His "Incalculable" Influence on Others: Essays on Robert Frost in Our Time

English Literary Studies
University of Victoria
1994

ENGLISH LITERARY STUDIES

Published at the University of Victoria

Founding Editor
Samuel L. Macey

GENERAL EDITOR
Robert M. Schuler

EDITORIAL BOARD
Thomas R. Cleary
Evelyn M. Cobley
Kathryn Kerby-Fulton
Victor A. Neufeldt
Stephen A. C. Scobie

ADVISORY EDITORS
David Fowler, *University of Washington*
Donald Greene, *University of Southern California*
Juliet McMaster, *University of Alberta*
Richard J. Schoeck, *University of Colorado*
Arthur Sherbo, *Michigan State University*

BUSINESS MANAGER
Hedy Miller

ISBN 0-920604-78-1

The ELS Monograph Series is published in consultation with members of the Department by ENGLISH LITERARY STUDIES, Department of English, University of Victoria, P.O. Box 3070, Victoria, B.C., Canada, v8w 3w1.

ELS Monograph Series No. 63
© 1994 by Earl J. Wilcox
Cover photograph by courtesy of Lesley Lee Francis

CONTENTS

INTRODUCTION:

Robert Frost and the "Anxiety of Influence"

Earl J. Wilcox

Robert Frost had entered the American national consciousness as a kind of preeminent presence well before he was asked to write a poem on the occasion of the inauguration of John F. Kennedy in 1961. A unique honor had been accorded the poet on his seventy-fifth birthday when he received formal felicitations from the United States Senate. (Later, President Kennedy was to send the poet on a goodwill mission to the Soviet Union where he had a lively conversation with Nikita Khrushchev.) Thus, by the time Kennedy was elected, Frost was widely accepted both by the academy and by mass popular culture as the unofficial poet laureate of the United States. Frost's popularity and high standing have arguably never been achieved by another poet except perhaps Robert Penn Warren, who was named the "official" Poet Laureate of the United States in 1985. Frost's appointment as Consultant in Poetry to the Library of Congress (1958-59) had been tacitly agreed upon by all as tantamount to acceptance of his supremacy in American letters. Frost's stature was also reflected in part by the three dozen honorary degrees he had received from colleges and universities throughout the United States and abroad. Other accolades suggesting his estimable place in American culture and the literary canon were the Pulitzer Prize, awarded four times, and the distinguished Bollingen Prize for Poetry. His name appeared perennially, at least in the press, among those being nominated for the Nobel Prize for Literature.

Frost's place in the popular American consciousness has been traced in my essay, "The Curious Case of Robert Frost," where I show that between 1915 and 1980 more than three hundred articles focusing on Frost and his poetry appeared in popular journals such as *Reader's Digest* and *The Saturday Evening Post*. This media popularity corresponds to the fact that Frost was without equal in being in demand on the academic lecture circuit during the last two decades of his life. It has become commonplace during the three decades since his death to see almost daily lines quoted or paraphrased from the poet's most accessible poems in advertisements for computer companies ("take the road less traveled," reads one blurb), for sporting goods, for musical events, and an array of other business and cultural events. It seems obvious that Frost remains in the American consciousness in a deep and potent dimension.

Yet for all his eminence, Frost's stature as a poet among the "moderns" is still being argued. In general, critics now agree that he has a good deal more in common with Eliot, Williams, Stevens, and other modernists and postmodernists than had been earlier perceived.

In addition to discussion about Frost's place as a "romantic" or "modern" or "postmodernist," two other significant issues remain largely unsettled: a definitive biography and his influence on other poets. Biographical studies in the 1980s by William Pritchard, George Monteiro, and Stanley Burnshaw have provided valuable standards by which the authoritative life may yet be written. More recently, another prominent Frost scholar and a granddaughter of the poet, Lesley Lee Francis, has written a fascinating study of the Frost family during the 1912-14 period. Based on hitherto unknown notebooks and a little magazine produced by the Frost children, *The Frost Family's Adventure in Poetry* portrays the Frost family as close-knit, a view one does not find in Lawrance Thompson's biography.

The collection of essays presented in this book examines the most challenging issue as yet unaddressed: the influence of Robert Frost on other poets. It is not the intention here, however, to respond *per se* to questions raised about the influence enigma in modern criticism. Harold Bloom's *The Anxiety of Influence* has illuminated thinking on the topic as perhaps no other study has done in our time. On the other hand, Bloom's own summary provides an avenue by which one might pursue issues raised by the presence of Frost in the American mind:

> If this book's argument is correct, then the covert subject of most poetry for the last three centuries has been the anxiety of influence, each poet's fear that no proper work remains for him to perform. Clearly, there has been an anxiety of style as long as there have been literary standards. But we have seen the concept of influence . . . alter with the post-Enlightenment dualism. Did the anxiety of style change also even as the anxiety of influence began? Was the burden of individuating a style, now intolerable for all new poets, so massive a burden before the anxiety of influence developed? When we open a first volume of verse these days, we listen to hear a distinctive voice, if we can, and if the voice is not already somewhat differentiated from its precursors and its fellows, then we tend to stop listening, no matter what the voice is attempting to *say*. (148)

Bloom's argument here is a succinct but forceful statement delineating both the dilemma and the requirement that all strong-voiced poets (Bloom's *Apophrades* or "strong dead poets") will always influence others. The significance of Bloom's designation of "strong dead poets" for Frost is that until very recently he was dismissed as a "weaker" poet—one whose own style would never "return" from the dead, one whose poetry, in Bloom's terms, would not be in poems "as in our lives," and would most surely "not come back [to "darken"] the living" (Bloom 139). Stated in another way, the debate over whether Frost belongs with the "moderns," "romantics," or "postmoderns" is unsettled precisely because he has had a pervasive influence on a wide range of poets as different as Wilbur, Dickey, Roethke, Rita Dove, Jarrell, Dana Gioia, Maxine Kumin, and James Wright. It should come as no surprise, then, that Frost's "return" has manifested itself in far more subtle ways than in the selection of a New England setting or a speaking idiom, to name only two superficial methods by which Frost's influence has often been measured. Speaking of Frost's self-assured yet self-critical art, Robert Hillyard perhaps said it best when he claimed that "the effect of his influence is incalculable" (see Peter J. Stanlis's essay, below). Despite Frost's enduring presence, the pervasive influence of this "strong dead poet" has not heretofore been studied in any detail. These essays seem especially timely in light of the New Formalist movement whose aim is to restore metrical poetry to a higher status than verse has held since the "invasion" of free verse. Frost's equivocation on the question of free verse and his own "anxiety" about how his poetry might be read as free verse add new dimensions to the study of issues such as a "national style." The essays in this book do not, however, generalize about Frost's influence; rather, each essay addresses specific ideas and forms in which one may see the relationship of Frost to individual poets with whom Frost has much in common.

The Essays

When the notion for this collection surfaced, the names of poets from across the English-speaking world who reflect Frost's influence were suggested—names such as John Berryman, Robert Francis, William Meredith, Robert Graves, Robert Lowell, Edward Thomas, Seamus Heaney, Maxine Kumin, Dana Gioia. On reflection, however, essays focusing on these poets were not included because a consistent theme linking them to Frost seemed lacking. What follows, instead, is a gathering of essays (only the first of such studies, one hopes) which shows forcefully that Frost's presence in the American consciousness permeates both the popular and the intellectual dimension.

The "national style" of the "anecdotal, plain-spoken lyric" owes much to Frost, Jonathan N. Barron claims in his essay, "Robert Frost and a New Tradition." Richard Wilbur and Rita Dove are two poets who reflect this "national style," which is signaled by the facts that both have won major prizes, publish with major presses, and have appeared in the popular press. Frost's "Design" bears a striking relationship to Wilbur's "First Snow in Alsace" and to Dove's "The Great Palaces of Versailles," verifying Barron's thesis that an intricate counterpoint links the three poets.

The flowering in the early nineties of the New Formalism reminds sages everywhere that there is nothing new under the sun. Perhaps this kind of shock of recognition was precisely what allied Randall Jarrell to Robert Frost, even if the two seemed worlds apart in their poetry. Richard Calhoun demonstrates in his essay, "'A Unique Natural Phenomenon Beyond Good and Evil,'" that Jarrell found the "authentic Frostian voice" when he began rereading Frost in 1947 for a review of *Steeple Bush* for *The New York Times Book Review*. This exercise marks the beginning of Jarrell's change of mind about Frost, a change that led to the discovery of "something reassuring about [Frost's] poetry, . . . almost like prose." This discovery undoubtedly bonded Jarrell to Frost, and in his subsequent criticism Jarrell "was more sensitive to Frost as poet than [Lawrance] Thompson could be or even [William] Pritchard chose to be." Calhoun also hears strong resonances of Frost in Jarrell's own poems, such as "A Country Life," "Moving," and especially "Woman."

If Jarrell discovered his affinities with Frost as both a poet and critic, it was Theodore Roethke who "looked to Frost as an ancestor in the tradition of poet-teachers, and defined and shaped himself in relation to the older poet," claims Pamela Davis. In her carefully concatenated essay, Davis argues that both poets "taught by talking." In doing so, Frost demonstrated his belief that "thoughts, like poems," were "momentary stays against confusion." Evidence suggests that Roethke knew and thought about Frost's methods "as early as graduate school," though the two poets were at polar odds in their attitudes toward teaching. Frost's approach was detached and rational, Roethke's engaged and intuitive. "Expansion of being rather than expansion of intellect is Roethke's main goal as a poet and teacher, and the main quality that sets him apart from his ancestor Frost." Roethke also believed that Frost's poems were "implicit with self-congratulation," and that his "method of educating by poetry leaves out love." Roethke's "A Light Breather" can be seen as taking up Frost's challenge "to make the final unity" of matter and spirit, and the younger poet's "The Voice" can be read as a direct response to Frost's "Oven Bird," as Roethke reshapes Frost's views on the teacher-poet to suit his own.

Not only celebrated contemporaries such as Jarrell and Roethke were drawn into Frost's network of poets, critics, and teachers. Robert Hillyer (1895-1961) and Robert Frost had, according to Peter J. Stanlis, a "forty-five year unbroken friendship," and that relationship resonated deeply throughout the sixteen volumes of poetry and other influential books that Hillyer published during his lifetime. It was Hillyer who proclaimed as early as 1933 that Frost is "our greatest living American Poet," and that the "effect of [Frost's] influence is incalculable." Like many poets since (such as Robert Lowell, Galway Kinnell, Richard Wilbur, and William Jay Smith), Hillyer celebrated Frost's friendship and inspiration, particularly in "A Letter to Robert Frost" (1934), an epistolary poem of 221 lines that pays "tribute to Frost's greatness as a poet, conversationalist, and teacher." Stanlis shows that the two poets shared common traits such as their conservatism in religion and politics, and their conception of society and human nature. At the same time, Hillyer and Frost generally wrote very different kinds of poems and seem to have shared very little in personal temperament. Theirs was indeed an interesting friendship.

The sixteen volumes of Hillyer's poetry stand in obvious contrast to the smaller number of volumes produced by his more famous friend. Still another contemporary, Mark Van Doren, published more than twice as much poetry as Frost. Always described as a follower of Frost, Van Doren himself won a Pulitzer Prize and had a distinguished career as a teacher, poet, and critic. Mordecai Marcus argues that, among other things, the poets "shared a joy in existence in the face of inexplicable griefs and uncertainties, and a determination to go on to the end, pursuing the light ahead." Van Doren's "moderately" successful poems show Frost's influence most obviously: "Former Barn Lot," "Dispossessed," and "Ambush" are conspicuously Frostian in treatment and situation, but they lack the sharpness, deftness, and conviction of Frost's poems. Van Doren's finest poems, both early and late, "echo Frost's idioms as well as his temperament." Among these are "Autonomous" and "Wish for the World." In the latter poem are "strong echoes of Frost poems extending from 'The Trial by Existence' through 'Birches.'"

As is obvious by now, many modern American poets have apparently come to grips with how they feel toward Robert Frost; James Dickey is one who has explored his feelings publicly and rather fully, in both an essay-review and a lengthy interview. Donald J. Greiner points out these connections between Frost and Dickey, but also concedes that most readers of "twentieth-century American poetry are not likely to think of the [two poets] together." What the two share, however, is "an unusual affinity with nature, an ability to look, to see something in the landscape besides the merely human." In this seeing, both Frost and Dickey discover "the gulf between the human endeavor and the non-human other." Individual poems such as Frost's "Design" and Dickey's "The Other" suggest that Frost's influence on Dickey is "largely a matter of Dickey's reaction against Frost's and the modernists' 'indoorness,'" as Dickey himself has confirmed.

As we have seen above, Robert Hillyer and Mark Van Doren shared common ground in their relationship to Frost in that both were influential poets, critics and teachers. Yet they remain minor poets. However, two younger contemporaries, Richard Wilbur and William Jay Smith, are major American poets who sustained important relationships with Frost and whose work resonates with Frost connections. Dorothy Judd Hall explores these resonances in her important essay, "Narrowing Our 'Soul-From-Soul Abyss': Inward Journeys of Robert Frost, Richard Wilbur, and William Jay Smith." Hall examines affinities of "interiority" through analyses of Wilbur's "The Mind-Reader," Smith's "Journey to the Interior," and Frost's "Directive." Hall suggests that Frost's interiority "resembles a Möbius strip—circling back toward its starting point yet somehow turned upon itself—rather than a purely inward vector." A significant sign connecting Frost with Wilbur can be seen most clearly, Hall shows, in the shared geode image. Finally, Hall believes the two poets are linked in concepts such as "suffering" and "the mind-of-God," concepts reflected in both Wilbur's "The Mind-Reader" and Frost's *A Masque of Reason*. These and other poems, Hall believes, show that both poets are "ontotheological." Smith's debt to Frost is reflected most compellingly in his poem, "Journey to the Interior," where "Smith has captured the darker truth hidden in Frost's poem ["The Road Not Taken"]: that all our short-range options grow increasingly illusory the closer we come to the end of our course."

If Henry David Thoreau is the New England writer to whom Frost owes much for an appreciation of nature, then Wendell Berry is the modern poet who is most often thought to owe his love of nature to Frost. Ed Ingebretsen, in "Robert Frost's 'The Pasture' and Wendell Berry's 'Stay Home': Figures of Love and the Figure the Poem Makes," explores the relationship of the "mutuality of love and poetry" in the two poets. Both writers combine the "agrarian" and the "human," and Frost's "The Pasture" and Berry's "Stay Home" connect to show that "love emerges as Frost's most well-imagined symbolic space." Berry's "long view of the historicity of human love," furthermore, "develops Frost's insight that literature . . . is one debt we owe to those who have gone before us."

Some poets pay their homage to Frost by writing a poem to him, some by their choice of subject matter or style. Others, such as James Wright, are even more direct. Of his 1957 volume in the Yale Series of Younger Poets, Wright said, "I've tried very hard to write in the mode of Robert Frost . . ." Peter Stitt, in his essay, "James Wright and Robert Frost: Debts and Diversions," discusses Wright's subsequent acknowledgments of Frost's influence. Stitt presents Wright as "the major American nature poet of his generation, and in this respect . . . the natural heir to Frost." The impact of Frost upon Wright was crucial, one sees, though finally Frost and Wright came to separate conclusions about "the frontier between nature and the metaphysical." Their differences become clear when poems such as Frost's "Design" and "Once by the Pacific" are compared with Wright's "The Minneapolis Poem."

Undoubtedly the most widely-known poem of homage to Robert Frost is Galway Kinnell's "For Robert Frost." Nancy Tuten, in " 'For Robert Frost': Form and Content in the Poetry of Galway Kinnell," examines ways in which Kinnell shows an understanding both of himself and the influence Frost had on his poetry. Tuten cites Frost's famous essay, "The Figure a Poem Makes," connecting it twenty-two years later with Kinnell's response to the charge that his own poetry "seemed more tentative than affirmative." While Kinnell eschewed the cultivation of form for its own sake, Tuten sees in Kinnell's tribute to Frost "a clear understanding of— and even a respect for—what language and form meant to the elder poet." And again, while seeing rhyme-schemes as limiting, Kinnell is drawn to the idea that a pre-determined form can lead to discoveries. Hence he sees Frost, in his best poems, coming "out with mysterious utterances that surprise even him. There is a lot of control and deliberate technique in most of his poems, but this doesn't stop him from making sudden frightening probes into the unsayable." In the long run, Frost's courage to probe "the dark woods" links him to Kinnell, as both poets recognize "the value of language as a means of dealing with life."

Afterword and Acknowledgments

As I have earlier suggested, this collection may be a harbinger of other explorations of Robert Frost's deeply resonating presence in modern American poetry. With the advent of the New Formalism and the spate of books and essays the movement seems sure to engender, one feels safe in saying that Frost's poetry and prose will be given new attention. Poetry may once again be examined not for its political correctness, its gender issues, or its rhyme or rhythm. Instead, poetry may once again be looked at as a figure that "begins in delight and ends in wisdom," a figure Frost claimed helped with "a momentary stay against confusion." If Frost's poetry has had this sort of influence on modern poets, he has indeed made a lasting impression on the American mind. We believe these essays demonstrate that, as critic Mark Scott has said, "Frost never sleeps for the poets."

I express my appreciation to several people without whom this collection would not have been attempted, refined, and completed. George Montiero's sessions for the Robert Frost Society (New York, 1992) provided a lively discussion of the topic, and some of the participants in these sessions are contributors to the present volume. My thanks go also to my colleagues in the Robert Frost Society who have been supportive in the endeavors of the Society since its inception. I thank also my colleague Jeffrey Glasgow of Winthrop University for his assistance in reading and editing the book and for his own "incalculable" influence in helping shape this and other new Frost studies. I thank Cheryl Hingle of Winthrop University for assistance in help with preparation of the manuscript. Special thanks are due to Sheila Neely, without whose constancy and good-spirited tenacity this book would still be buried in a word processor somewhere. Appreciation also goes to the many Frost scholars everywhere who have encouraged me in the task of putting together this collection. I regret that exigencies of space and time prevented the inclusion of many other excellent essays on the topic. And I thank Lesley Lee Francis for providing the photograph of Frost used on the cover and for granting special permission for its use here. Finally, I thank Elizabeth H. Wilcox, my first and best editor and colleague.

WORKS CITED

Bloom, Harold. *The Anxiety of Influence.* New York: Oxford UP, 1973.

Francis, Lesley Lee. *The Frost Family's Adventure in Poetry: Sheer Morning Gladness at the Brim.* Columbia: U of Missouri P, 1994.

Wilcox, Earl J. "The Curious Case of Robert Frost." *McNeese Review* 31 (1984-86): 3-13.

Robert Frost and a New Tradition

Jonathan N. Barron

Robert Frost is alive and well and living in contemporary poetry.[1] A mere glance at the contemporary scene tells us that of all the modernists from the early decades of this century, Robert Frost continues to exert a profound and widespread influence. In fact, his influence is so enormous that his poetics currently *defines* what I call our national poetic mode. I call this poetry "national" only because it has already been judged as such. A look at any of the following contemporary anthologies offers us well over a hundred poets working in the mode first set forth by Frost: *The Harvard Book of Contemporary Poetry, New American Poets of the 90s, The Morrow Anthology of Younger American Poets.*[2]

Most critics of twentieth-century American poetry tend to ignore or dismiss the role of Robert Frost in that poetry. Marjorie Perloff explains why this is the case in an essay, "Pound/Stevens: Whose Era?"[3] There, she explains that critical argument concerning the influence of the century's early poets divides into a party advocating the centrality of Pound (Hugh Kenner) and a party advocating the centrality of Stevens (Harold Bloom). Perloff explains that "a concordance of Stevens criticism, if there were such a thing, would probably show that the following words had a very high incidence: *being, consciousness, fiction, reality, self, truth.*" She adds, "Certainly they are not the words we meet in discussions of the *Cantos.*"[4] Perloff suggests that the study of twentieth-century American poetry depends on two mutually exclusive paradigms: Romanticism and postmodernism. "If Poundians take MAKE IT NEW! as their watchword, one might say, without being at all facetious, that those who regard Stevens as the great poet of our time admire his ability to MAKE IT OLD."[5] Perloff then explains that William Carlos Williams was the one poet of the early twentieth century who could link these two differing aesthetics. In her discussion of the critical debate over twentieth-century poetry, Perloff does not mention Frost. This may be due to her willingness to conflate Romanticism with modernism; however, there are many reasons why one should be wary of such combinations, not the least of which is the fact that the poetry of Robert Frost calls into question the relationship between such terms as Romanticism and modernism. After all, his work is as unlike both Stevens and Pound, as Stevens and Pound are unlike each other. Yet, like both of those poets, Frost continues to exert a strong influence on the contemporary poetic scene.

Frost's innovations have exerted such authority that, today, his aesthetic has become the dominant national mode, an aesthetic mode I call "Romantic Modernity." I use this term because, on the one hand, Frost writes in a Romantic idiom developed by Wordsworth, while, on the other hand, he manifests a twentieth-century skepticism. As in Wordsworth's, the philosophical center to Frost's poetry is the autonomous individual; and, like Wordsworth, Frost wrote measured poetry according to traditional English prosodic rules. Also like Wordsworth, Frost pushed those rules to new limits. But unlike Wordsworth, Frost follows in the wake of Darwin, Marx, and Freud. His poetry makes use of an ironic, skeptical, self-conscious, detached voice as it explores the issues raised not only by that intellectual triumvirate but also by such twentieth-century thinkers as Einstein, Heisenberg, and Niels Bohr. Read for what he says, Frost must be considered a modernist. But read for how he says it, Frost appears to be a Romantic. Frost criticism itself splits along these very lines, with one group reading Frost the neglected modernist and another reading Frost the latter day Romantic.[6]

Poets, however, have long recognized that Frost's strength comes from his ability to be both Romantic and modern at once; specifically, they are attracted to his poetics which manages to create a modern poetry out of Romantic material. Before explaining how contemporary poets use Frost's innovations, I want to identify just what constitutes a special "Frostian" poetics in the first place. Thematically, Frost's poetry explores the moment of crisis when the very idea of autonomy is thrown into radical doubt by some encounter with an Other, what theorists refer to as "the sublime."[7] Wordsworth, too, was interested in this intersection between the autonomous individual and the world outside. In this sense, Frost's sublime poetry also attempts to preserve the autonomous self from those outside systems which might threaten it. But Frost asserts his modernity when his poetry describes the individual's resistance to the specific twentieth-century social and scientific paradigms which challenge the very idea of autonomy. Frost's poetry, then, is a defensive poetry designed to preserve the value of individual agency, of autonomy, against anything social or natural that might threaten it.

Frost made this defense in a specific prosodic form. He used a narrative lyric poem which employed demotic diction, the rhythms of spoken language, and the traditional rules of English prosody. Although this may appear to be like the Wordsworth of *Lyrical Ballads*, Frost wanted his poetry to go "beyond" Wordsworth; he wanted it to be even more literal, even more faithful to the sound and rhythm of everyday speech than Wordsworth's poetry. "As language exists in the mouths of men, here again Wordsworth was right in trying to reproduce in his poetry not only the words—and in their limited range, too, actually used in common speech—but their sound."[8] When Frost made his poetry conform to the rhythm and sound of the spoken word, he defended his own autonomy against the larger "tradition" of English poetry itself. As he said: "I alone of English writers have consciously set myself to make music out of what I may call the sound of sense."[9] Frost calls for the artist to pay attention, at the level of the sentence, to the meaning inherent in sounds alone. In this regard, he speaks like a modernist; he speaks like Pound or Williams. But like his Romantic predecessors, Frost refused to write poetry without some traditional metrical system. To his mind, as to Wordsworth's, a poet's originality (a poet's autonomy) emerged not from new metrical inventions but from the ability to make "the sound of sense" come through, "across" a pre-established metrical system.[10]

Frost's poetics, his Romantic Modernity, combines a close attention to the aural quality of language with a single-minded adherence to the value of the autonomous individual and human agency. This combination of style and theme creates what looks like a simple poem: the diction is simple, and the story appears to be straightforward. Those who do not attend to the formalist, prosodic fireworks in Frost's poetry assume the poems to be naive and simplistic. And those who fail to examine the import of the stories told see rather straightforward narrative events with little philosophical import. But the conjunction of style to theme, of the sound of demotic speech to a story of individual autonomy, actually makes for a highly sophisticated, philosophically rich poetry. To paraphrase the late Mayor Daly's complaint to the Chicago press corps, Frost's poems rarely mean what they say, and too many people confuse what they say with what they mean. As Frost himself once said with regard to poetic theory, "I am not undesigning."[11] One might offer this as the motto for today's Frostian poets.

As I have mentioned, contemporary Frostian poets continue to dominate the national literary life. A brief list of recent Pulitzer Prizes, for example, reveals a shockingly similar poetic—similar, that is, when compared to the radical innovations of Charles Bernstein, on the one hand, or the highly wrought couplets and ornate diction of Frederick Turner on the other. Both Turner and Bernstein, it should be said, make it quite clear in their prose as well as their poetry that they write in reaction to Romantic Modernity; they mean to resist the dominance of the personal, anecdotal, plain-spoken lyric—the Frostian poem.[12]

Just as the poets in the avant-garde, the "Language" poets and the "New Formalists," attack such work,[13] so, too, have many leading critics of contemporary poetry. Their chief complaint is that such poetry is nothing more than a plethora of sentimental anecdotes. This criticism, made by Charles Altieri, Marjorie Perloff, and Walter Kalaidjian, tells us that such poems are flat, fluffy, and anti-intellectual.[14] Because such poetry continues to be read without the benefit of Frost's aesthetic of Romantic Modernity, such dismissive and negative conclusions will continue to be drawn.

I propose, then, that we read the plain-spoken lyric not against the work of Pound, Stevens, Williams, or even Eliot or Stein, but rather that we read these lyrics against the equally original and important aesthetic innovations of Robert Frost. In the following pages, I will examine Frost's "Design,"[15] and follow that discussion with a look at two poems which exemplify the current forms of the contemporary aesthetic mode of Romantic Modernity. The first poem, by Richard Wilbur, defends the autonomous individual by breaking a new demotic diction across an old meter. The second poem, by Rita Dove, defends the autonomous individual in a newly invented poetic form that breaks with traditional meter in order to more accurately portray human speech.

In "Design," even as Frost plays with the inherited "design" of the sonnet, he maintains a simple diction that counteracts both the intricate formal gestures and the philosophical, ethical heart of the poem. Glancing at the form, we find that instead of two quatrains, the octet has a hidden, third quatrain between the dashes of lines 3-6. And, instead of the usual number of rhymes that we expect in sonnets, Frost uses three. But then there are only three characters: spider, heal-all, and moth. The form, therefore, replicates the subject, hiding itself just as the two white insects hide on the white flower. The diction, meanwhile, deceives us as well, because the simple language leads us to believe that the poem tells a simple story. As Marie Borroff carefully details, Frost's diction, in general, is amazingly free of latinate and others complex words.[16] But this simple diction works in ironic counterpoint to the story. This poem charts the moment of crisis which overcomes the speaker once he realizes that his own sense of "autonomy" may be a fiction. If "design govern in a thing so small," then might not the speaker, too, be governed as well? Is he as autonomous as he would like to believe?

This question arises in the last line, "If design govern in a thing so small." The meter is regular, the diction is simple, but the arrangement is not. Although that line concludes a couplet, the couplet itself is broken by both a question mark and a dash. Also, the tone of the line is not decisive—as we would expect from a traditional couplet—but ambiguous. In other words, one can read the last line as a question, even though it is punctuated as a statement. Ultimately, that line does not look away from the poem—it does not give us a moral to think about. We are not asked to think about Darwinian design, nor are we asked to think about a religious teleological design. Instead, that line forces us to look once more at the poem, as a poem, as a small design, as a sonnet, an artifact. And once we do that, we must acknowledge the autonomy and agency of Frost himself.

To raise the issue of design, in other words, is to ask about the designer. In the case of Frost's poem, to raise the issue of design is to acknowledge two interpretations of the natural and human world: Darwinian and Christian. When the poem speculates that even the most minute event is "governed," it raises the question: who governs? Is this a story of natural law, or is it a story of "God's plan." In either case, in either story, the poet's autonomy, his agency, will be erased. The achievement of the last line, then, is to re-direct the reader's eye back to the artifact of the poem and so to the artificer, the poet. Once re-directed, we notice that Frost, as poet, resists the hegemonic power of the sonnet form itself by adding a quatrain and destroying a couplet. More than that, we notice that, in this poem, Frost asserts his ability to question not only the law of poetry, but the law of God, and the law of nature as well.

This, then, is the "witches' broth" (line 6) of Romantic Modernity which Frost bestows on contemporary American poetry. In that broth we have a demotic diction which is meant to be heard spread across a complex formal structure which is meant to be read. We also have a philosophical defense of autonomy based on the poet's ability to create the poetic structures themselves. In this poem, then, Frost tells us that the human power to design and to re-design can be a force of resistance when faced with systems that might overwhelm the human subject.

Romantic Modernity of this sort—combinations of simple diction, complex formal gesture, common subject matter, and the philosophical exploration of the meaning of autonomy—have continued in American poetry from the beginning of the postwar period until the present day. If one judges by the major university presses, New York commercial publishers, Pulitzer Prizes, and the commercial and literary press, then, the most awarded, most typical contemporary poetry is the Frostian poem of Romantic Modernity. The poems one is most likely to see in *The New Yorker*, *The Atlantic*, and *Harper's* (to take but three commercial and literary magazines) are poems which focus on the resistance of single characters to those larger forces that would inscribe them. Also, the poems in those magazines often avoid excessive rhetorical display and complex diction in favor of a straightforward demotic imitation of speech.

As an example of Frostian poetry that continues to make use of traditional prosody, I turn to Richard Wilbur's 1947 "First Snow in Alsace." There, we find a disturbing story told in simple diction, a story which questions the meaning of autonomy itself. Specifically, the poem describes snow which falls on a battle-field and covers the dead even as it covers "children's windows" (line 12).[17] This image once again raises the issue of design. Wilbur's implicit question, posed in the form of a statement, however, is even more haunting than Frost's: Wilbur wonders who it is that creates such images; he wonders who it might be that can associate the snow falling on corpses with the snow falling outside a child's window. He discovers that he, the individual, makes these designs. And he defends this move, this aestheticization of death, as a necessary statement of autonomy and personal freedom.

The speaker tells us: "the ration stacks are milky domes; / Across the ammunition pile / The snow has climbed in sparkling combs" (lines 10-12). In this image, the descriptive language of the Romantic poet is joined to the World War II image of ammunition piles and ration stacks. The conjunction creates a verse that is not only overwritten, but horribly out of place. What kind of person would describe such artifacts in such language? Wilbur answers this implicit question in the following lines: "You think: beyond the town a mile / Or two, this snowfall fills the eyes / Of soldiers dead a little while" (lines 13-15). In these lines, the "false" diction of "milky domes" and "sparkling combs" is pared away. In its place, we are given the demotic language of the soldier. But the eyes that could see a "milky" beauty in the ammunition are the same eyes, the same "you," that see snow falling on the dead. A Frostian poet must deny the beauty of the "milky domes" because the language itself is false. The diction does not represent the experience. Wilbur's speaker, however, can look, as it were, beneath the diction. Although he expresses the beauty of the snow on the ammunition, this sight leads inevitably to the imagined sight of snow on the bullets' victims. The false diction, the beauty, forces the speaker to "think," and, in thinking, he sees the dead soldiers blinded, first by the bullet, and then by the snow.

The poem plays the false Romantic diction—"milky domes"—against what Frost called "the sound of sense," the actual spoken rhythms and words of people—"this snowfall fills the eyes." In so doing, Wilbur suggests that the same man who used false language to express the beauty of snow did not regret the beauty that he saw. Rather, he simply became more honest; he explains, in the more direct speech of a twentieth-century soldier, that he also sees beauty in the more graphic image of a corpse. The poem implicity asks why it is that when "this snowfall fills the eyes / Of soldiers dead a little while" it is still an image of beauty and not of horror.

In the concluding lines to the poem, Wilbur suggests that the ability to see beauty, the ability to create aesthetic artifacts even out of death, is not a problem to address. Rather, it is proof of one man's ability to assert his individual strength and autonomy. Wilbur makes this point when the night guard retreats to a time when, as a child, he was the first to see the snow: "The night guard coming from his post / Ten first snows back in thought, walks slow / And warms him with a boyish boast: // He was the first to see the snow" (lines 22-25). As in so many of Frost's New England poems, here a man wonders if it is possible to conjure up a time when things, even if they were illusory, appeared real. The child's first sight of snow is no less genuine, and no less beautiful, according to this poem, than the sight of snow on dead men. Just as the child could thrill to the power of his own ability to be the first to see, so can the man thrill to his ability to see. As if in homage to Frost, we are told that on those children's windows the "frost makes marvelous designs" (line 21). Intended or not, this allusion is perfectly placed in a poem about the individual's ability to make cruel associations, an ability that would endorse the power of the individual over any system that might subsume him.

In these concluding lines, Wilbur accents the night guard's ability to aestheticize even the most disturbing image in order to accent his ability to do something outside of a wartime context. If the night guard can remove himself from a landscape of death, then he can assert his power over the forces that created that landscape in the first place. If the night guard can find beauty as an experiential fact and not as a naive Romantic image of "combs," then, he can validate his own autonomy in his own experience. The night guard asserts his own agency when he demonstrates his ability to see outside of the context that would limit him: he can see beyond what Jerome McGann would call the Romantic Ideology of "milky domes," and he can see outside the context of the killing fields.[18] But even this assertive power is ambiguous. The last line—"He was the first to see the snow" (line 25)—is set apart from the rest of the poem and so breaks the stanza pattern. But it breaks only the poem's pattern, not its meter. Joined and yet distant, this line emphasizes the double nature of "firstness." The guard was the first to see the snow, so he thought, as a child. Now, he is the first to see it as a man. But the moral cost of seeing the snow in a new context, in war time, might be to associate with enemies beyond one's control. There is a moral ambiguity in the last line which might explain why it is separated from the rest of the poem. Although this poem suggests that some reading can literally preserve one's own private sense of humanity, the metrical link binding the last line to the rest of the poem ties the very ideal of the poem to an earlier Romantic paradigm; it forces us to wonder about rather than celebrate those who feel the need to see snow on a corpse as a thing of beauty.

In the late 1950s, after Wilbur published this volume, poets who defended the autonomous self in lyrics that emphasized the lived, aural, demotic, plain-spoken "sound of sense" began to ignore the rules of English prosody. In his 4 July 1913 letter to Bartlett, Frost said, "But if one is to be a poet he must learn to get cadences by skillfully breaking the sounds of sense with all their irregularity of accent across the regular beat of the metre."[19] By the late 1950s, poets who continued to be interested in Romantic Modernity began to ignore "the beat of the metre" in favor of their own organically derived "beats." They developed what in the 1960s was known as "Naked Poetry." Once the iron law of traditional prosody had been broken, Frostian poetry gained a new "free verse" form; it was freed from the law of traditional meter but still liable under the laws of Frostian Romantic Modernity.

Today, then, there are two distinct aesthetic routes that Frostian poets can follow. They can make traditional prosody new, as Frost did throughout his career, or they can make their own unique new prosody Frostian. No doubt Frost himself would be unhappy with those who eschew traditional metrics altogether, but that does not make the poetry of such poets any less "Frostian."

Rita Dove is one such "free verse" Frostian poet. In her 1987 Pulitzer Prize-winning volume, *Thomas and Beulah*, she tells the story of an individual who insists on her autonomy in the face of such larger systems as race, class, and gender. Using a demotic language that emphasizes the rhythms of speech, Dove is one of the most important poets writing in the free verse form of the Frostian mode of Romantic Modernity. Few of Dove's poems repeat any one metrical unit or syntactic unit in any regular pattern: they are free verse. But most of Dove's poems do incorporate the main elements of the Frostian aesthetic.

In "The Great Palaces of Versailles,"[20] we learn the story of Beulah, an African-American woman who works in Charlotte's Dress Shoppe in 1946 Akron, Ohio. In the first two lines, the poem introduces two systems which will deny Beulah's autonomy: "Nothing nastier than a white person! / She mutters as she irons alterations" (lines 1-2). Thinking about race—"nothing nastier"—Beulah quickly discovers that the female body is inscribed by gender codes as well—"she irons alterations." As she works on the clothes that help define the female body, she then considers the luxurious clothes and people of pre-revolutionary France. These thoughts occurring in 1946 introduce a historical contrast. In 1946 Beulah is, from the perspective of civil rights legislation, in a decidedly pre-revolutionary America thinking about pre-revolutionary France. She also thinks of "the white girls" (line 12) laughing in the next room, and in particular of one girl, Autumn, who laughs in "imitation of Bacall" (line 15). Beulah connects these girls to the French aristocrats who were able to hide their bodily functions so well that they "dropped excrement as daintily / as handkerchiefs" (lines 21-22). Beulah, ironing the alterations that will hide the peculiarities of the individual body, notes the separation between herself and Autumn. Beulah's body is marked by class—she works in the back room—and by race—she is black. The two identities keep Beulah apart from the white girls in the next room. Unlike those girls, however, Beulah can, like Wilbur's night guard, see things outside of the context that would confine her. Acknowledging those confining forces—in particular the racial codes that would mark her and a class system that will not promote her—Beulah is also able to acknowledge a gender code that is invisible to white girls like Autumn. We are told: "Beulah remembers how / even Autumn could lean into a settee / with her ankles crossed, sighing / *I need a man who'll protect me* / while smoking her cigarette down to the very end" (lines 34-38). In other words, Beulah remembers that even though Autumn may be privileged by her body—her white skin and wealth grant her more power than Beulah—she, too, must submit as a woman to men.

Beulah understands what Autumn cannot; she knows that the aristocratic code defining the needs of women is derived from the movies of Bogart and Bacall, movies which tell her that she "needs a man." Like the night guard's in Wilbur's poem, and like Frost's in his own "Design," Beulah's ability to see through the smallest detail, her ability to understand the meaning of a white girl's laughter, becomes an assertion of her individuality, and of her autonomy. As with both Frost's and Wilbur's poems, however, there is ambiguity in Dove's poem, too. We find ourselves wondering just how much autonomy Beulah does assert. For it may be that Beulah is twice alienated here. It may be that she envies Autumn's ability to enjoy the aristocratic life, to smoke a cigarette down, to sit in a settee and think about a man. Why should she not envy such a condition when stuck in the back of an Akron dress "shoppe" in 1946? In either case, the poem is still about autonomy, either its assertion or its loss. The fact that this story of potential resistance is told in a simple diction which

23

emphasizes the rhythms of spoken language makes this poem, like Wilbur's, Frostian.

These are but two examples of today's widespread national poetic style, the anecdotal, plain-spoken lyric. We can see why this style should be called national, when we recall that both poets, Richard Wilbur and Rita Dove, have won Pulitzers, have been published by prestigious New York presses, and have even appeared in the popular press. Wilbur was almost literally crowned in 1987, when he was made poet laureate, an honor that got him into *People* magazine. In that same year, Rita Dove won her Pulitzer. In 1993, she, too, was crowned poet laureate and appeared in *Time*. With the aid of Robert Frost, I propose that we learn to read both poets not as representatives of a failed anecdotal, plain-spoken lyric but as practitioners of a still unacknowledged, intellectually vibrant poetry of Romantic Modernity.

The strongest criticism against such work declares it to be in bad faith. Even as it claims to address the importance of human agency and the importance of autonomy, it actually asserts the deadening Romantic Ideology. Such is the claim of Annabel Patterson in her reading of Frost.[21] Like those critics (Kalaidjian, Altieri, Perloff) who dismiss the contemporary Frostian lyric, Patterson asserts that while Frost *does* manifest an annoying tendency to raise historical, political, even philosophical issues, in the end, his poetry evades and elides those issues. But that reading takes into account only the Romantic Frost. In his aesthetic which is designed to champion autonomy, there is more to evasion than meets the eye.

Frost's, Dove's, and Wilbur's common people, like the characters of other Frostian poets, find themselves in difficult circumstances that challenge their faith in their own agency. When people in difficult circumstances become the subject in poetry, the poem inevitably invokes social and historical events; we expect something to be said about them. But Frostian poets ironically change the focus, and so change our expectations as well. Rather than tell us what to think about the issues which threaten the agency of their characters, these poets tell us what they, or the character, did *because* of those issues. How does Beulah react to her situation in 1946? How does the night guard deal with the emotions brought about by the first snow in Hitler's Europe? In both cases they assert their own interpretive power to see beyond the very systems that might limit and define them. What one reader might label evasion, another more Frostian reader can label strength. After all, if we assume Beulah's situation to be real, what *can* she do, besides think her own way out of the prison house of confining systems? From that perspective, these poems are perhaps more honest that those that pretend to make something happen.

The typical Frostian poem, then, focuses on the response made by a given individual when faced with a challenge to his or her autonomy. The poem does not concern itself with the challenge; rather it concerns itself with what Wordsworth called the "obstinate questions" that such challenges provoke. These questions express the Frostian poets' faith in the freedom of individuals to resist the ideologies that would interpolate them. Currently, of the many modes of poetry available, only the Frostian poets dramatize the power inherent in evasive tactics, the power latent in the ability to question. In times of pervasive orthodoxies and clever certitudes, it is a good thing we have such poets among us still.

1 Standard works that help define the term "contemporary" are Richard Gray, *American Poetry of the Twentieth Century* (London: Longman, 1990); Alan Shucard, Fred Moramarco, and William Sullivan, *Modern American Poetry: 1865-1950* (Boston: Twayne, 1989); David Perkins, *A History of Modern Poetry*, 2 vols. (Cambridge: Harvard UP, 1976, 1987). The history of the contemporary period can be found in such works as Paul Breslin, *The Psycho-Political Muse: American Poetry Since the Fifties* (Chicago: Chicago UP, 1987); Robert Von Hallberg, *American Poetry and Culture: 1945-1980* (Cambridge: Cambridge UP, 1985); James E. B. Breslin, *From Modern to Contemporary, American Poetry, 1945-1965* (Chicago: Chicago UP, 1984).

2 *The Harvard Book of Contemporary American Poetry*, ed. Helen Vendler (Cambridge: Harvard UP, 1985); *New American Poets of the 90s*, eds. Jack Myers and Roger Weingarten (Boston: Godine, 1991); *The Morrow Anthology of Younger American Poets*, eds. Dave Smith and David Bottoms (New York: Morrow, 1985).

3 *The Dance of The Intellect* (Cambridge: Cambridge UP, 1984) 1-32.

4 Perloff 9.

5 Perloff 14. Perloff agrees with Bloom that modernism is but a late manifestation of Romanticism. Modernism, she argues, still adheres to a faith in the interior, autonomous subject. It is only the postmodern poet, such as Pound, who finally breaks with this code. See "Postmodernism and the Impasse of the Lyric," in the same volume (172-200).

6 Frost's role as a modernist is, at best, uncertain. Critics, after all, have given us equally good reasons to see him as both a modernist and a Romantic. See Richard Poirier, *Robert Frost: The Work of Knowing* (New York: Oxford UP, 1977), and *The Renewal of Literature: Emersonian Reflections* (New York: Random, 1987), especially 147-81; Frank Lentricchia, *Robert Frost: Modern Poetics and the Landscapes of Self* (Durham: Duke UP, 1975). More recently, Robert Kern took up Lentricchia's argument in "Frost and Modernism," *American Literature* 60 (1988) 1-16.

7 There is an extensive body of work on the relationship between "the sublime" and poetry, a subject that has engaged some of the leading theorists of the contempo-

rary period: De Man, Derrida, Lyotard, and more recently Slavoj Zizek who examines "the sublime" and film.

8 Interview in the *Boston Evening Transcript,* May 8, 1915; rpt. in Elaine Barry, *Robert Frost on Writing* (New Brunswick: Rutgers UP, 1973) 153-54.

9 Letter to John Bartlett, 4 July 1913, *Selected Letters of Robert Frost,* ed. Lawrance Thompson (New York: Holt, Rinehart and Winston, 1964) 79.

10 For more close analysis of Frost's poetic theory see John F. Sears, "Robert Frost and the Imagists: The Background of Frost's 'Sentence Sounds,'" *The New England Quarterly* 54 (1981) 467-80. Also see the following essays: Eric W. Carlson, "Robert Frost on 'Vocal Imagination, the Merger of Form and Content,'" *American Literature* 33 (1961-62) 519-22; Robert S. Newdick, "Robert Frost and the Sound of Sense," *American Literature* 9 (1937-38) 289-300; Tom Vander Ven, "Robert Frost's Dramatic Principle of 'Oversound,'" *American Literature* 45 (1973-74) 238-51.

11 *Selected Letters* 84.

12 Bernstein, *Contents Dream* (Cambridge: Harvard UP, 1984); Turner, "Mighty Poets in their Misery Dead" in *Poetry After Modernism,* ed. Robert McDowell (Brownsville, OR: Story Line, 1991), 342-73. For a discussion of what's wrong with this national mode from the perspective of New Formalism see Wyatt Prunty, *"Fallen From the Symboled World": Precedents for the New Formalism* (New York: Oxford UP, 1990), and Robert Richman, "Poetry and the Return to Seriousness," *New Criterion* (1985) 39-48.

13 I do not include the New Formalist poet in my definition of the Frostian lyric. In particular, I do not include those who write polemics against that lyric, poets such as Dana Gioia, Brad Leithauser, Wyatt Prunty, Frederick Turner. Their overarching concern with matters formal often leads to the sort of ornate diction and subject matter that Frost and his followers seek to challenge. Frost, in short, wrote the antidote to the lush poems of Rupert Brooke. If such lushness now returns, we should not confuse it with Frost.

14 Perloff, *Radical Artifice* (Evanston: Northwestern UP, 1990); Altieri, *Self and Sensibility in Contemporary American Poetry* (Cambridge: Cambridge UP, 1984); Kalaidjian, *Languages of Liberation: The Social Text in Contemporary American Poetry* (New York: Columbia UP, 1989).

15 *The Poetry of Robert Frost,* ed. Edward Connery Latham (Boston: Holt, 1969).

16 *Language and the Poet: Verbal Artistry in Frost, Stevens, and Moore* (Chicago: Chicago UP, 1979).

17 First published in *The Beautiful Changes and Other Poems* (New York: Harcourt Brace, 1947) and available in *New and Collected Poems* (New York: Farrar, Straus, Giroux, 1987) 347.

18 See Jerome McGann, *The Romantic Ideology* (Chicago: Chicago UP, 1983).

19 *Selected Letters* 80.

20 *Thomas and Beulah* (Pittsburgh: Carnegie-Mellon UP, 1987) 63-64.

21 "Hard Pastoral: Frost, Wordsworth, and Modernist Poetics," *Criticism* 29 (1987) 67-87.

"A Unique Natural Phenomenon Beyond Good and Evil": Randall Jarrell on Robert Frost

Richard J. Calhoun

My interest in the influence of Robert Frost on Randall Jarrell comes in part from an advantageous perspective as a graduate student in Chapel Hill at a time in the 1950s when Frost visited every spring, while Jarrell, at the nearby Woman's College of the University of North Carolina in Greensboro, was the prototypical poet-critic. I also believe that Jarrell is, at the moment, a much undervalued critic. At Chapel Hill then, Frost would meet with small groups of students for informal talks in preparation for a public "saying" of his poems before large audiences. I was never privileged to attend the annual after-reading party and ritualistic early "breakfast" hosted by the English faculty. I was, however, fortunate to be a graduate student host for a reading in the 50s by Jarrell at which he indicated his developing interest in Frost. On rare occasions in those days I would see his sports car parked outside Kemp's record store in Chapel Hill. I even put my hands on a Mahler recording he had selected for himself and was politely but firmly told by the bearded and instantly recognizable Jarrell to "desist." It was no matter: a man who looked every inch a poet and who liked both Frost and Mahler could not, in my opinion, go far wrong.

Frost was induced, on at least five occasions in the 1950s, to travel thirty-five miles for readings in Greensboro, where Jarrell always had prepared his students with elaborate introductions to his own favorite Frost poems.[1] At Chapel Hill, no graduate student ever thought to ask Frost what he thought of Jarrell's poetry or his essays on Frost in *Poetry and the Age*, well thumbed by those of us who sought a less impersonal and judgmental critical alternative to the New Criticism.[2] It did not seem quite safe to bother Frost with questions about other living poets when he was himself the main event.

It is my contention that an accounting of the relationship of Frost and Jarrell can tell us something consequential about the growth of Frost's critical reputation in the 1950s, as well as something about his largely unacknowledged and inadvertent influence on younger poets in the furtherance of what we know now as postmodernism. If a poet of Jarrell's or Lowell's generation wanted a different poetic father from Eliot or Allen Tate, Williams, as is well known, and Frost, as is less established, were the exemplars to whom to turn. Frost was of special value to a poet like Jarrell, who wanted something different from standard modernism but wished to continue with the traditional forms.

Their first encounter began unpromisingly. In the fall of 1937, Robert Frost came to Kenyon College to read his poetry, on the invitation of President Gordon Keith Chalmers. Sharing John Crowe Ransom's attic were a transfer student from Harvard named Robert Lowell and a newly appointed part-time instructor of English and "director of tennis," Randall Jarrell, a favorite student of Ransom at Vanderbilt, who had followed him to Kenyon. William Pritchard reports, he believes on the authority of Robert Penn Warren, a minor incident Jarrell created after Frost's reading.[3] I heard in the early 60s a version of the same incident from Mrs. Roberta Schwartz Chalmers, the wife of President Chalmers, attesting that what was said had some import for those who heard. At the party following his reading, Frost, holding forth on metrics, looked around the room for agreement with his views. Jarrell in his often rather high-pitched voice was heard to say, "I don't agree with that." Frost, not prone to hear what he did not want to, talked on.

It is not surprising that a young and brash Randall Jarrell would not honor Frost's dictums at that time. Jarrell's critical views had been seasoned in the Vanderbilt of the New Critics. The chief advocate of modernism was the man that both Lowell and Jarrell accounted their mentor, Allen Tate. Anyone who ever had proximity to Tate would testify that his was a hard influence to withstand; he did not tolerate desertions from the formalist cause. Witness his unrelenting contempt for Lowell's new style in *Life Studies*.[4] For a rebellion against this literary father only the example of a great poet would suffice. For Jarrell, Frost became that poet.

Jarrell's temperament as critic was based on strongly stated views which accommodated loosely disguised personal contradictions. His demeanor was very much that of a well-read professional critic, but he was actually a scholar-athlete with surprisingly popular tastes. If Rilke, Eliot, Williams, Stevens, and Frost were his heroes, so was Johnny Unitas of the Baltimore Colts; and Jarrell's passion was almost as much for tennis as for poetry.

Jarrell was also equivocal about modernism in literature and formalism in criticism. His career owed much to the New Critics. His great benefactor Ransom saw that he was published in the *Kenyon Review*. The first issue of Brooks and Warren's *Southern Review* included two of his poems. Jarrell had understood the significance of writing in the modernist tradition, but his own personal inclinations were often not towards the kind of poetry the magazine bastions of the New Criticism were nurturing. The most appropriate term I can use to describe the realization that Jarrell came to from reading Frost is Edmund Wilson's use of Melville's phrase "the shock of recognition." He found, through rereading the poetry of William Carlos Williams and Robert Frost, sanction from a dependency on Tate, as well as exemplars for his own parting from modernism in poetry and formalism in criticism. Jarrell admired less their "art" than the "real life" he found in their poetry. Above all he liked their ability to convey a sense of voice, their regard for good talk. Like his friend Robert Lowell, Jarrell began to covet the freedom to explore a more natural, less artificial style for his own poetry, something more like prose. Frost had always been there for Jarrell to discover, but it was not until the late 1940s that Jarrell made that discovery, experiencing something of his own "shock of recognition."

Jarrell's schooling in Frost began in 1947 when he reread him for a review of *Steeple Bush* for the *New York Times Book Review* and to prepare a summer lecture at Indiana University on Frost's poetry. It was during this rereading that Jarrell did something rare: he changed his mind, but the change was not evident enough for Kathleen Morrison to show the review to Frost. What is usually remembered from this review is Jarrell's lament: "most of the poems merely remind you, by their persistence in the mannerisms of what *was* genius, that they are productions of somebody who once, and somewhere else, was a great poet."[5] Part of the review is concerned with identifying what Jarrell believed critics did not like, the public Frost as actor. Although he had not yet adequately identified "the other Frost" he was beginning to appreciate, he does recognize a poem that served as a tribute to the genius that had been, "Directive." He only mentions some of the earlier poems for which he would later express his appreciation—"Home Burial," "A Servant to Servants," "Design." He identifies Frost's major accomplishment in the face of modernist impersonality, complexity, archetypes and myth: "no other living poet has written so well about the actions of ordinary men" (142).

Another thing happened to Jarrell on the road away from modernism towards postmodernism. New Directions publisher James Laughlin asked him to write an introduction to William Carlos Williams' *Selected Poems*. In his *Autobiography* Williams declared that the success of Eliot's *The Waste Land* had delayed twenty years the poetry "in the American grain" he was trying to foster. A crucial discovery of the 1950s in which Jarrell was a leading player was that for a tradition "in the American grain" there were Frost, Williams, and before either of these, Walt Whitman. For a brief moment after World War II (before the Korean war, before the trauma for intellectuals of the election of Eishenhower and the defeat of the erudite Adlai Stevenson, and before the advent of McCarthyism), intellectual America felt good about itself. Consequently, there was much more than just a touch of literary nationalism in what Jarrell and other critics like Karl Shapiro found in turning to the Americanness of Whitman, Williams, and Frost. Even Eliot and the major-phase Henry James were claimed as "American" or attacked as too European. D. H. Lawrence's *Studies in Classic American Literature* was rediscovered. William Pritchard documents that Jarrell became fond of quoting Marianne Moore's phrase, "plain American that cats and dogs can read."[6]

The Frost that Jarrell proclaimed for the fifties in *Poetry and the Age* was not quite that "plain," but he was the Frost the younger poet needed —"The Other Frost," a popular poet who had not been seen for the real artist he was, a poet who could earn the wider audience that prose writers enjoyed and modernist poets had lost. Jarrell wrote: "there's something reassuring about his poetry, . . . almost like prose."[7] The early modernist desire for poetry to be at least as well written as prose was back. Lowell had already sought this effect in *Life Studies*. Jarrell had discovered another Frost for critics and poets writing in the later stages of modernism. "Besides the Frost that everybody knows there is one whom no one even talks about" (26). Jarrell wanted to be the first critic to talk about this poet, his "other Frost." But to do so, he has to exorcise the public Frost everyone thought he knew, "The Farmer-Poet," or as he said it in Jarrellese, "a sort of Olympian Will Rogers out of *Tanglewood Tales*" (26).

Jarrell knew that he must replace "their" Frost, the poet of both the sentimentalizers and of the formalists, with "his" Frost, establishing that "Frost's best known poems, with a few exceptions, are not his best poems at all" (27). "The other Frost" is no alienated modernist but a poet more in Williams' "American grain" who makes the reader feel that he is "not in a book but in a world, and a world that has in common with his own some of the things that are most important in both." Jarrell's critical taste then stands the test of forty years of time now: the poems of "the other Frost" happen to be those in vogue today.

In a longer essay in *Poetry and the Age*, "To the Laodiceans" (that is, addressed to Frost's only lukewarm followers), Jarrell contests an attitude dating from "the days when 'serious readers of modern poetry' were most patronizing to Frost's poems."[8] He could have specified F. O. Matthiessen and Marxist critics, neohumanists like Yvor Winters, but also formalists like R. P. Blackmur and Cleanth Brooks and Allen Tate before they began to see some merit. Prior to *Poetry and the Age* a critical taste for Frost would have raised serious doubts about one's seriousness as a scholar and critic, or as a serious graduate student, as I discovered at the Kenyon School of English in 1949, by defending Frost in the presence of Yvor Winters and Allen Tate, an episode still too painful to recount. Jarrell endeavored to find in Frost at least some of the tensions needed for a poet to be acceptable to the New Critics. His "other Frost" was a poet who exhibited "seriousness and honesty," "craft" and "real people," "real speech," "real thought," and "real emotions," all performed with subtlety and exactness. When I first read Jarrell's *Poetry and the Age*, I wished I had had his book a few years earlier at Kenyon. I knew I had found in the 50s, the critic who had made a case for Frost. On rereading Jarrell in the 90s, I was surprised to see how much of what we say about Frost now, Jarrell said then, how much I had credited as originating with Poirier, Brower, or even Trilling's notorious 85th-birthday tribute was at least presaged by Jarrell.

In *Poetry and the Age* Jarrell writes as a poet-critic for whom Frost's best poetry, read properly, became a pretext for his own dissatisfaction with modernism and served as an tacit bridge to postmodernism. Something new was needed. The "regular ways of looking at Frost" have kept us from "seeing Frost for what he really is" (35). Critics ought to know his best poetry and to find "some other way of talking about his work," just as poets like Jarrell and Lowell, at the apparent end of modernism, need to find another way of writing. Jarrell admits even a "new" criticism of Frost may not do justice to "the range and depth and height of his poems," but if Jarrell is only allowed to "appreciate," "the poems speak for themselves almost as well as poems can" (36). It was this appreciative aspect of Jarrell's criticism that struck a responsive chord in many of his readers.

Still one has to know, as Jarrell does, that poems he identifies as the "Yankee Editorialist side of Frost" get "in the way of the real Frost, of the real poems and real subject matter" (37). Jarrell's judgment as to which poems to read is still apropos to our 90s benchmarks because he had detected much of the authentic Frostian voice, discovering how Frost says things "with flat ease," how he "takes everything with something harder than contempt" (39). He finds a bona fide complexity here, a characteristic "recognition of the essential limitations of man, without denial or protest or rhetoric or palliation" (39). In commenting on "Directive" Jarrell identifies "three of Frost's obsessive themes—those of isolation, of extinction, and of the final limitations of man" (46). "Desert Places" is judged "a poem almost better, at the same game, than Stevens' beautiful 'The Snow Man'" (57). Jarrell even acknowledges Frost's sexuality in "The Pauper Witch of Grafton" and in "The Subverted Flower," proclaiming there is "more sexuality in these poems than in several hothouses full of Dylan Thomas" (56). Much of what Jarrell "recognized" then we now know through later critical manifestations in Poirier, Brower, Elaine Barry. What we can still learn from revisiting Jarrell is his insistence that "Frost is sometimes a marvelous rhetorician, a writer so completely master of his own rhetorical effects that he can alter both their degree and kind almost as he pleases" (49). We need to recognize that "Frost is that rare thing, a complete and representative Poet"—a great and subtle craftsman (61).

I have a personal interest in Jarrell's third remarkable essay on Frost, "Robert Frost's 'Home Burial,'" since his second reading of this essay, after Johns Hopkins, was at my invitation at Clemson. He wrote to me of his essay on "Home Burial" and its approaching publication in Don Cameron Allen's *The Moment of Poetry* and asked if he might give it again, since he had read it only at Hopkins as a Turnbull lecture.[9] I was impressed on hearing it then, and still believe today that it remains an exemplary close reading of a long poem and establishes that Jarrell was much more than an inspirational appreciator, at his best a great critic. I would highlight two things that Jarrell does better here than anyone else has since: his focus on what the repetitions reveal about the drama of "Home Burial," and his demonstration of how the poem first implies attitudes that are later made explicit. Jarrell explores brilliantly the dramatically intricate meanings of what the characters say. He distinguishes the poem as a family tragedy, in which the husband, after the death of their child, senses that he is being shut out of his nuclear family, pleading from his sense of exclusion, "give me my chance." The poem designates a "home burial with a vengeance," with the house invaded by the "stains" from the burial of the dead child, and then zeroes in on the key word—"apart." It is the wife, sensitive to the solitariness of the grave, who would choose to stay "apart" from her husband and from the "way of the world." No one makes as much as Jarrell of the way "you" is said by both the wife and the husband at the end of this poem or explains more convincingly why the man's last words have to be "by force. I will."

The three essays I have discussed—"The Other Frost," "To the Laodiceans," and "Robert Frost's 'Home Burial'"—are Jarrell's major contributions to Frost criticism, mentioned by later critics but not as thoroughly appreciated as they should be for how assertive they were at that time in describing another Frost. In them I recognize the origin of many of our current basic assumptions about Frost. I would also reclaim a fourth essay: Jarrell's Frost canon should include his 1957 *New York Times Book Review* piece on *A Swinger of Birches: A Portrait of Robert Frost* by Sidney

Cox.[10] A decade after his first critical interest Jarrell is ready to proclaim Frost, not Stevens or Williams, "the best poet alive." He likes Cox's emphasis on Frost and play, which Jarrell recognizes as often serious play, and again appreciates "The Subverted Flower" and "The Pauper Witch of Grafton."

Jarrell's final word on Frost was his almost unnoticed 1964 *Herald Tribune* review of Lawrance Thompson's *Selected Letters of Robert Frost.*[11] He did not live to have his say on Thompson's biography, but he does note Thompson's revelations of the differences between the public and the private Frost. Jarrell, the reviewer, is more exonerating than the official biographer was to be: "It is so wonderful to read Frost—was so wonderful to get to see and hear him—that we forget how hard it was to be Frost" (365). His judgment is understanding and compassionate: Frost's public self was the result of the "terms of his armistice with the world." He notes what is evident from his understanding of the real complexities of the poems: there was a devil in Frost that defeated his intentions.

Jarrell writes perceptively of Frost, and, implicitly, of his own growing anxieties about his own career: "Just under the skin of the stocky, rock-faced old success—a great celebrity and a greater poet—the thin, sensitive-faced young failure survived" (366). He continues: "Frost wanted to be convinced not that he was good, but that he was a good poet; and it took all the laughter and applause of audiences and friends, all the love and admiration plain in their eyes, to persuade him of this" (367). He adds a quote from Frost: "My whole anxiety is for myself as a performer. Am I any good? That's what I'd like to know and all I need to know" (368). Jarrell sums up: "But, of course, no artist can ever know this about his own work" (368). He identifies the fear Frost felt in his last years: "the best we have to offer 'may not be found acceptable in Heaven's sight'—the work can fail like the life" (368). Jarrell is more sensitive to Frost as poet than Thompson could allow himself to be or even Pritchard chose to be. For Frost and for Jarrell as poets, such matters were crucial because, as Jarrell concludes, "Between the darkness and chaos visible outside, invisible inside, the poet and his poems stand in ordered concentration." In my judgment this review is a final insightful essay on Frost, poet and man, and a projection of Jarrell's own doubts. For Jarrell, who was to lunge before a car in the falling dusk on a highway outside Chapel Hill, Frost's letters may have also been a personal shock of recognition of the anxieties of a poet.

In the twilight of modernism Frost criticism needed Jarrell, and Jarrell's poetry needed Frost's example. Critics in the later 1950s were beginning to look for something more personal, even to detect "a distinctive voice" in a poet they championed. Leslie Fiedler was one of an increasing number who had concluded that Jarrell had none; if so, Frost was obviously a poet who did.[12] As early as 1948-49, Jarrell had given up his planned book on the American modernist and once friend of Allen Tate, Hart Crane. In the 1950s he turned away from the modernists to writing on two poets not yet fully accepted by the establishment, Williams and Frost, and one whose greatness was only recently being recognized, Wallace Stevens. He even broke off personal correspondence with Tate and picked a public argument with the reputable modernist critic, R. P. Blackmur.

Probable Frostian influences begin appearing in Jarrell's poetry, most specifically in poems like "A Country Life," "When I was Home Last Christmas," "Moving," and especially in the poem "Woman" and in his sensitive treatment of women in other poems. This was a subject that Jarrell wanted to question Frost on, as evidenced in the his Library of Congress interview of Frost—how to characterize, how to "create" women in poetry. Jarrell's poetry, especially as his regard for women in *The Woman at the Washington Zoo* suggests, became especially indebted to Frost's *North of Boston*. His sympathy for women was kindled by Frost's observation that "the woman always loses, but she loses in an interesting way. She pulls the whole thing down with her."[13] Jarrell had found an important subject but could not quite manage the "interesting way" with Frost's realism. In a few of his poems like "Next Day," Jarrell did manage to realize in his own poetry some of the play he found in Frost. The older poet's example was now always there to urge Jarrell toward "talk" and "the sound of sense" without resorting to free verse. The most perceptive thing that Pritchard says about Frost and Jarrell comes from his brief attempt to relate Jarrell to Derrida and his followers, in their "privileging of speech over writing."[14] The influence in this privileging should be identified as the example of Frost.

After the publication of *Poetry and the Age* in 1953, Jarrell was arguably the most influential man of letters in America. And central to his reputation as a critic were his essays on Frost, whose critical reputation was at last becoming commensurate with his popular following. By 1954 Robert Penn Warren had praised and even Allen Tate had complimented Frost's poetry. Brooks and Warren had recorded an interview with Frost on metrics, and it was widely distributed on a Holt, Rinehart and Winston tape. But no one contributed in the 1950s to Frost's reputation more significantly than Randall Jarrell. For Frost to be fully acceptable, the "other Frost" had to be presented. There was even a shrewdness on both sides in the relationship of Frost and Jarrell about their mutual indebtedness. Jarrell needed the Frost that he saw in the best poetry in order to certify his break with New Critical tenets and modernist poetic practice. He knew what he had done for Frost and understood what Frost thought of him. He even detected some of the character flaws in Robert Frost that Thompson was to flag and Helen Vendler to use in her famous review of Thompson, "a monster of egoism." But Jarrell understood both the poet and the man. In a letter he designated Frost as "a unique natural phenomenon beyond good and evil," hardly the position Lawrance Thompson was to take.[15] He confided to Lowell that he existed for Frost as "the person who'd written those pieces about his poetry." He continued:

> He felt I was an Indian who'd sold him, *given* him Manhattan Island, and he was willing to keep me on a special little reservation in return. (483)

Mary Jarrell has divulged that when Robert Frost read in Greensboro, Randall Jarrell elaborately prepared his students for Frost's coming by teaching poems that Frost never read publicly, "Home Burial," or seldom read, "A Servant to Servants"; one might say all the wrong poems for the public occasion. It was Jarrell's own idea of Frost that he prepared his students for, his "other Frost." Clifford Lyons, Frost's friend from Florida days, was his host in Chapel Hill. He would drive Frost over to Greensboro, and Jarrell would usually drive him back after the reading and early morning "breakfast" meals that would follow Frost's evening readings.

There is no record as to what they talked about after those readings. I did unearth one account from Greensboro of what Frost said on the last of those trips back to Chapel Hill from Greensboro, however. Jarrell was unable to drive Frost back, and Lyons could not come and get him. A junior faculty member eagerly volunteered to make the trip. If Frost did not know you, conversation was not easy. After stark silence, at some time during the ride back, Frost spoke: "This Randall Jarrell. I have never read his poetry. Is he any good? I have often wondered." They drove on into the night. We know from his criticism that Jarrell knew Frost was good.

NOTES

[1] My sources for much of this material include correspondence with the late Clifford Lyons of Chapel Hill, Bob Watson in Greensboro, and a conversation with Mary Jarrell after a session on Jarrell at Chapel Hill.

[2] Randall Jarrell, *Poetry and the Age* (1953; rpt. New York: Vintage, 1955).

³ William H. Pritchard, *Randall Jarrell: A Literary Life* (New York: Farrar, Straus and Giroux, 1990) 49-50.

⁴ Iran Hamilton, *Robert Lowell: A Biography* (New York: Random House, 1983) 236-37.

⁵ Randall Jarrell, "Tenderness and Passive Sadness," in *Kipling, Auden & Co.: Essays and Reviews 1935-1964* (New York: Farrar, Straus and Giroux, 1980) 140-42.

⁶ *Randall Jarrell: A Literary Life* 160.

⁷ "The Other Frost," in *Poetry and the Age* 26-33.

⁸ *Poetry and the Age,* 34-62.

⁹ "Robert Frost's 'Home Burial,'" Don Cameron Allen, ed., *The Moment of Poetry* (Baltimore: Johns Hopkins, 1962) 99-132.

¹⁰ "In Pursuit of Beauty," in *Kipling, Auden & Co.* 275-76.

¹¹ "Good Fences Make Good Poets," in *Kipling, Auden & Co.* 365-68.

¹² Leslie Fiedler, "Some Uses and Failures of Feeling," *Partisan Review* 15 (August 1948) 926.

¹³ Jarrell's interview for the Library of Congress, *Robert Frost Interviewed by Randall Jarrell, in the Recording Laboratory, 19 May 1959,* Magnetic Tape T 2849 (formerly, LWO 2849).

¹⁴ Pritchard 215.

¹⁵ Mary Jarrell, ed., *Randall Jarrell's Letters* (Boston: Houghton Mifflin, 1985) 482.

Teacher-Poets: Robert Frost's Influence on Theodore Roethke

Pamela Davis

Robert Frost told a reporter in 1960 that "the three strands" of his life were "writing, teaching, and farming." People have always been interested in how two of the strands—farming and writing—are linked. But what about writing and teaching? How are they interwoven? This is the question that drew me into a study of how Frost's identity as a teacher-poet both infused his work and influenced teaching poets who came after him.

In the generation after Frost, arguably the most important poet-teacher was Theodore Roethke, a figure whose influence continues to be felt in the poet-teachers working today. Roethke, always deeply concerned with ancestors, looked to Frost as an ancestor in the tradition of poet-teachers, and defined and shaped himself in part in relation to the older poet. Together these two men stand as important pillars in a lineage of U.S. poet-teachers, a lineage that I believe is a significant and largely unrecognized one in the history of American poetry. It is, in effect, a tradition of poetry that comes both out of an impulse to teach and from strong convictions about how teaching and learning are accomplished. Ultimately, these poets' identities as teachers (identities which were, by the way, firmly in place well before they became known as poets) shaped their poetry in profound ways. Frost even said, "It slowly dawned on me that my poetry and my teaching were one, and if you know my poetry at all well, you'd see that" (Hewlett 176).

Frost and Roethke shared many of the same ideas about education and the educational value of poetry. But more important than their similarities are their differences. What I want to do here is to describe Frost's theories and methods of education, connect these to his poetry briefly, then show how Roethke both assimilated and revised these theories and methods in working out his own identity as a teaching poet.

Many students, observers, and friends have described Frost's teaching style, and their observations come to this: Frost taught by talking—expansively, spontaneously, and on a wide range of subjects. For Frost, talking was thinking. Essentially, he appeared in the classroom and started thinking aloud, moving his mind in and among whatever subjects arose, modelling for his students what one of them called "the energy of a mind thinking close to its subjects" (Craig 3). Frost not only modelled thinking, he modelled original thinking. As a teacher, he considered the capacity for original thinking one of the primary goals of education. For Frost, original thinking meant continuous thinking, thinking as an ongoing process in which thoughts are not stable and permanent, but in a constant state of evolution. Frost saw reality as formless and chaotic, and in order to handle that, one had to participate in constant ordering and reordering of this reality. Thoughts, like poems, were for Frost "momentary stays against confusion." Both thoughts and poems involved an act of making, active shaping of the raw material of ideas. Teaching for Frost was in essence a public performance of such activity.

Those familiar with Frost's statements on poetry are no doubt beginning to notice that the vocabulary one must use to describe his talking and thinking (i.e., his teaching) is very similar to the vocabulary he uses to describe his poetry. The words "original," "talk," "performance," "surprise" all appear in his statements on poetry. In essence, poetry for Robert Frost is like thinking, and since thinking is manifestly the same act as teaching, poetry is like teaching.

Not only is poetry *like* thinking, *like* teaching, however; it *is* thinking and it *is* teaching. For poetry also involved the fundamental element of thinking: making metaphors. Frost wrote, "Education by poetry is education by metaphor" (*Selected Prose* 35). He defines metaphor as "saying one thing and meaning another" (36) and then defines thinking as "saying one thing in terms of another" (41). Poetry acts as a teacher by making metaphors and thus showing people what thinking means.

The ability to make metaphors is the ability to use language in fresh new ways and new combinations, and this ability marks the free person. "The whole object of education," Frost told a group of Wesleyan students, "is to get freedom and give freedom, to enjoy freedom" ("The Manumitted Student" 5). Freedom means not having knowledge handed to you on a platter, but having rather the ability to think originally. Frost's definition of a schoolboy is often quoted: "One who can tell all he knows in the order in which he learned it" (*Selected Prose* 20). Elsewhere he said, "Total recall is slavery. Apt recall is freedom" (MS. 935940/4). Overall, Frost conceives of right education as producing original, thinking people who are free for productive, creative action. His teaching and his poetry both work in support of this multidimensional goal.

Theodore Roethke knew Frost's work from a relatively young age; in addition, there is evidence that at least as early as graduate school, he knew and had thought about Frost's methods and aims as a teacher as well as his methods and aims as a poet. Certainly Roethke identified Frost as one of the ancestors against whom he would measure and define himself as he pursued his twin passions of teaching and poetry.

Roethke's teaching style revealed his passionate commitment at every turn. He was deeply, almost obsessively involved in his students and in his classroom performances. Part of the reason that Roethke was so emotionally involved in his teaching was that he believed that learning was primarily a matter of feeling. Insistently, he urged the incorporation of visceral emotion into the learning process. Now Frost had certainly advocated the importance of emotion and of feeling one's rational knowledge to be true; Roethke, however, advocated attaining a kind of knowledge that went well beyond the rational. Roethke's goal for his students was to move them beyond the selves that were to the selves they could become. This educational goal is linked to his notion of poetry, which he defines at one point in his notebooks as "the dream of what we could be" (39.135). Poetry and education thus move us toward the selves we have the potential to be and know.

One of the most important ways we can expand our selves, according to Roethke, is to recover our lost capacity for creative thinking. He felt that good poetry, as the ideal manifestation of creativity, had enormous educational potential in the arena of developing creative thinking. "Even to hear a good poem carries us far beyond the ordinary in education," he wrote (*On the Poet and His Craft* 44).

Roethke's views on the educational value of poetry in certain regards coincide very closely with those of Frost. In short, poetry instructs in all the most important elements of thinking. First, a poem is a creative act that bears the personal imprint of the maker. Second, the thought in a good poem is, as Frost put it, "more felt than known" (*Selected Prose* 45). Third, Roethke believes with Frost that because it is based on metaphor, poetic thought is unique and original.

However, while agreeing that poetry teaches the desirable skill of thinking, the poets differ ultimately in their view of what it means to think and how people learn to think. For Frost, thinking is primarily a conscious, rational, intellectual process, a process of comprehension. For Roethke it is primarily a pre-conscious, intuitive, visceral process, a process of apprehension. This primary difference is reflected in the different teaching styles of the two poets.

While Frost's contact with young people remained at a somewhat detached level emotionally, Roethke's psychic involvement was so intense that it contributed to his frequent breakdowns. The contrast between the two poets is instructive in beginning to build up a picture of what Roethke reacted *against* in Frost. Frost advocated what he called "education by presence"—it was not his job to reach out to students, but rather theirs to reach out to him. This is at distinct variance with Roethke's style. Roethke's notebooks abound with entries related to the psychic dangers of teaching. He wrote, for example, "You can't go out all the way; therein lies madness and death. I insist that the teaching poet preserve his identity" (28.10). And elsewhere, "Teacher: one who lives with the young with such desperate intensity" (36.69). Still another entry reads, "In teaching, I have come to a kind of death" (44.221). Teaching represented a kind of death for Roethke in the same way that love did for a long time, a dangerous identity-threatening outreach into another soul. In fact, his notebooks contain much evidence that he understood his teaching to be an act of love. "I teach out of love," he wrote, "and let the Freudians do with that what they will" (34.42).

Overall, then, Roethke's approach to his students and his teaching was highly emotive and psychically charged, in sharp contrast to Robert Frost's more detached, rational style based on thinking and talk. Like his teaching, Roethke's poetry reflects his commitment to pursuing knowledge founded in feeling, intuition, and non-rational processes of mind. Much of his poetry appeals to the primitive language of the unconscious. Often instead of ordering chaotic reality in "momentary stays against confusion," Roethke chooses to participate in that chaos, to speak what he calls in one poem "the wild disordered language of the natural heart" ("Meditations of an Old Woman") and thereby expand his being. Expansion of being rather than expansion of intellect is Roethke's main goal as a poet and teacher, and the main quality that sets him apart from his ancestor Frost.

Scattered notebook entries suggest what Roethke primarily disliked about Frost. Roethke writes, "Many of Frost's poems are implicit with self-congratulation" (36). He exhibits the same discomfort with Frost's tone in these fragments from some teaching notes: "What bothers me, often, in Frost is the psychic stance: he is [a] mighty cozy character, tough and pleased with himself—his life and self-control" (68.10). Roethke perceives in the other poet an egotism, a satisfaction with his own being. He senses in Frost, perhaps, a stable identity such as he himself could never achieve and indeed would never have wanted, for such an identity implies smug removal from the forces of change and becoming.

Roethke, then, rebelled against Frost's detached rationalism, and even as he was influenced by Frost's view of thinking as making metaphors, he began to find the Frostian conception of metaphor as saying one thing in terms of another too thoroughly based in logic and intellect, too much a rational/intellectual game that the poet played with his readers. Instead of metaphors, Roethke turned to poetic figures that did not appeal to mind but to emotion, spirit, and the unconscious. These poetics figures can more accurately be called "symbols." Roethke's use of symbols rather than metaphors reflects his conception that the process of achieving understanding (i.e., the process of learning) occurs largely on a non-rational level. Frost's more frequent use of metaphors likewise correlates with his view that learning involves greater control over one's rational faculties—specifically the ability to use the mind to bring previously unassociated ideas together into unique combinations, or as he said, "to put two and two together."

This is not to imply, however, that Frost never used symbols, or that Roethke never used metaphors. In fact it is illuminating to examine cases where Roethke did work in metaphors, and to compare his handling of them with Frost's. One poem in particular—"A Light Breather"—seems to play quite directly with Frost's notion of metaphor and then move beyond it—always Roethke's favorite way to handle an ancestor.

> The spirit moves,
> Yet stays:
> Stirs as a blossom stirs,
> Still wet from its bud-sheath,
> Slowly unfolding,
> Turning in the light with its tendrils;
> Plays as a minnow plays,
> Tethered to a limp weed, swinging,
> Tail around, nosing in and out of the current,
> Its shadows loose, a watery finger;
> Moves, like the snail,
> Still inward,
> Talking and embracing its surroundings,
> Never wishing itself away,
> Unafraid of what it is,
> A music in a hood,
> A small thing,
> Singing.

This poem brings to mind a passage from "Education by Poetry" in which, speaking of metaphor, Frost said,

> The greatest of all attempts to say one thing in terms of another is the philosophical attempt to say matter in terms of spirit, or spirit in terms of matter, to make the final unity. That is the greatest attempt that ever failed. We

stop just short there. But it is the height of poetry, the height of all thinking, the height of all poetic thinking, that we attempt to say matter in terms of spirit and spirit in terms of matter. (*Selected Prose* 41)

With "A Light Breather," Roethke takes Frost up on this challenge. The way in which he says matter in terms of spirit and vice versa in this poem illustrates his own view of what is involved in the "height of all poetic thinking."

The poem's method is to begin with a simile for the spirit, and then extend the simile until it elides into metaphor. The poet uses three similes: the spirit stirs "as a blossom," it plays "as a minnow," and it moves "like the snail." He then transforms these similes into metaphors by combining a description of the spirit with descriptions of blossom, minnow, and snail in such a way that the spirit and the organic thing fuse: it becomes impossible to tell to which one—spirit or thing—he is referring.

In this metaphoric technique, Roethke does more than simply say one thing in terms of another, or say spirit in terms of matter. He actually makes one thing become the other, makes spirit become matter. By starting out saying X is like Y, and ending up making X and Y one and the same, his metaphors accomplish not just a process of thinking, but an actual process of growth. Spirit, blossom, minnow, and snail all end up more multidimensional than they started out.

Roethke's response to Frost, then, is that the attempt to say matter in terms of spirit and spirit in terms of matter is not doomed to failure if one realizes that more than philosophic thought is involved. Thinking is not enough to accomplish this greatest kind of metaphoric expression. The metaphor must be an act of growth and becoming as well as an act of thinking, for the fusion of spirit and matter cannot successfully take place at the level of intellect alone. Thus, to Frost's concept of metaphor as original thinking, Roethke adds a component of spiritual growth. If education by poetry is education by metaphor, Roethke thereby suggests that education is not just learning to think, but learning to become more than one was. From Roethke's point of view, Frost's method of educating by poetry leaves out, for the most part, any such education in spiritual becoming.

Roethke also felt that Frost's method of educating by poetry leaves out love. "The Voice" is Roethke's poetic confrontation with this perceived Frostian deficiency. With "The Voice," Roethke engages and answers Frost's poem, "The Oven Bird," suggesting in the process what he feels is missing in Frost's avian teacher figure. Here are the two poems in their entirety:

The Oven Bird

There is a singer everyone has heard,
Loud, a mid-summer and mid-wood bird,
Who makes the solid tree trunks sound again.
He says that leaves are old and that for flowers
Mid-summer is to spring as one to ten.
When pear and cherry bloom went down in showers
On sunny days a moment overcast;
And comes that other fall we name the fall.
He says the highway dust is over all.
The bird would cease and be as other birds
But that he knows in singing not to sing.
The question that he frames in all but words
Is what to make of a diminished thing.

The Voice

One feather is a bird,
I claim; one tree, a wood;
In her low voice I heard
More than a mortal should;
And so I stood apart,
Hidden in my own heart.

And yet I roamed out where
Those notes went, like the bird,
Whose thin song hung in air,
Diminished, yet still heard:
I lived with open sound,
Aloft, and on the ground.

That ghost was my own choice,
The shy cerulean bird;
It sang with her true voice,
And it was I who heard
A slight voice reply;
I heard; and only I.

Desire exults the ear:
Bird, girl, and ghostly tree,
The earth, the solid air—
Their slow song sang in me;
The long noon pulsed away,
Like any summer day.

"The Voice" takes the ingredients of "The Oven Bird"—bird, wood, tree, summer, diminishment, and song—and re-orders them to emphasize a wholly different perspective on the art of the poet teaching.

As many commentators have noted, another name for the oven bird is the "teacher bird." Here Frost's teacher-bird/poet conveys "facts" to the listener through his tone of voice. In Frost's poem, the teacher-bird has center stage. He is the one doing the talking, just as Frost, when he taught, was usually the one doing the talking. The bird's talk is addressed to a universal audience—"everyone has heard" him—and is loud enough to make "the solid tree trunks sound" in echo. The personality of this bird is the opposite of the one we encounter in Roethke's poem. Roethke's bird is "shy"; his song does not echo loudly off trees but is "thin" and hangs in the air "Diminished, yet still heard." This reversal is interesting. Now it is not the world that is diminished, but the bird's voice. In fact, from the poet's point of view the world is full and rich because his imagination, inspired by love, makes it so. "One feather is a bird, / I claim; one tree, a wood."

Roethke's bird singing with the true voice of the beloved, low yet partaking of a comprehensive truth, stands in marked contrast to Frost's bird, whose cry, not a song at all, is loud yet tells only of diminishment. Roethke moves his bird from center stage and makes it the voice of love—and with these two changes his bird becomes part of a world that both inspires and is unified by poetic creativity: "Bird, girl, and ghostly tree, / The earth, the solid air— / Their slow song sang in me." Again this unified world is the exact opposite of Frost's: in Roethke's poem the tree is ghostly and the air "solid." This suggests the transforming power of the voice of love, its ability to make the evanescent (air) tangible and knowable, and to make the known (tree) mysterious.

In another important reversal, Roethke emphasizes that the bird's and lover's voices are not heard by everyone, but, insists the poet, "I heard; and only I." The sound of truth, conveyed through love, can be heard only by the lover. The knowledge, illumination, and creativity he gains by hearing the song is personal and unique to him.

In both poems the birds' songs are inspirational, encouraging their listeners to make poetry and to use the imagination, but for Roethke an important source of inspiration is love, and so he adds that vital component to his bird's song.

While there is no way to prove a direct source for "The Voice" in "The Oven Bird," the correlations between the two poems are compelling. Roethke systematically changes those elements of Frost's poem that do not mesh with his view of what teaching and learning entail for the poet.

"A Light Breather" and "The Voice," then, confront Frost's perceived inadequacies in the subtleties of educating by poetry. These poems diverge from Frost's work exactly insofar as Roethke's beliefs about teaching and learning diverged from Frost's. Roethke deemphasizes the rational analytical faculties so important to Frost, and plays up the notion of teaching and learning as visceral, involving primarily emotional and non-rational faculties. He eschews the ideal that the teacher should remain above and detached from his subjects and his students, indicating instead his feeling that love and deep personal involvement are indispensable in a teacher. And finally, he insists that the act of teaching is always an act of learning, growth, and becoming, and never merely an act of telling.

WORKS CITED

Craig, G. Armour. "Robert Frost as a Teacher: An Address on the Seventy-Fifth Birthday of Robert Frost." 26 March 1950. MS. in Robert Frost Special Collection, Amherst College Archives.

Frost, Robert. "Commencement Address." Amherst College, 1935. MS. 935940/4. Frost Collection, Dartmouth College.

———. "The Manumitted Student." *The New Student* [Wesleyan College]. 12 January 1927.

———. *The Poetry of Robert Frost.* Ed. Edward Connery Lathem. New York: Holt, Rinehart and Winston, 1969.

———. *Selected Prose of Robert Frost.* Ed. Hyde Cox and Edward Connery Lathem. New York: Collier, 1966.

Hewlett, Horace W., ed. *In Other Words: Amherst in Prose and Verse.* Amherst: Amherst College, 1964.

Roethke, Theodore. *The Collected Poems of Theodore Roethke.* Garden City, NY: Doubleday, 1966.

———. *On the Poet and His Craft: Selected Prose of Theodore Roethke.* Ed. Ralph J. Mills, Jr. Seattle: U of Washington P, 1965.

———. Unpublished Notebooks. Roethke Collection, University of Washington.

Robert Frost and Robert Hillyer: An Enduring Friendship

Peter J. Stanlis

The forty-five year unbroken friendship of Robert Frost (1874-1963) and Robert Hillyer (1895-1961) began early in 1917, soon after Frost began teaching at Amherst College, and while Hillyer, his junior by twenty-two years, was an undergraduate at Harvard University. Hillyer had won a prize in poetry in 1916, and the first of his sixteen volumes of poetry was published in 1917. During his long friendship with Frost, he pursued a successful career in literature while teaching for almost forty years at Harvard, beginning in 1919. Among the highlights of his literary and academic life, Hillyer received a Pulitzer Prize in 1933 for his *Collected Verse*, and in 1937 he was appointed Boylston Professor of Rhetoric at Harvard. In 1938 he succeeded in having Frost elected to the Harvard Board of Overseers, and the next year he and David McCord arranged for Frost's appointment as the Ralph Waldo Emerson Fellow at Harvard.

In an epistolary poem of 221 lines, "A Letter to Robert Frost" (1936), against a background of criticism of contemporary literature and culture, Hillyer celebrated their close friendship, and paid tribute to Frost's greatness as a poet, conversationalist, and teacher. His monologue is in the tradition of Pope's "An Essay on Criticism" and "Epistle to Dr. Arbuthnot." The controlled couplet verse form, the sharp, sophisticated epigrammatic wit, and the deceptively understated tone and irony are touched with a modern idiom characteristic of Hillyer's reflective technique. In its tone and classical spirit it transcends Pope and is (as Frost would say) "like Horace in the true Horatian vein." These qualities appear in Frost's discursive philosophical poems, so that Hillyer's poem to Frost bears close critical comparison with the older poet's "New Hampshire," "Build Soil," and "The Lesson for Today."

Although it was not part of Hillyer's original general intention, "A Letter to Robert Frost," first delivered as the Phi Beta Kappa poem at Columbia University in June 1936, ironically served as an *apologia* for Frost's latest book, *A Further Range*, which had appeared three months earlier. The themes in Hillyer's poem regarding Frost's literary and cultural beliefs and achievements stood in stark and dramatic contrast to the barrage of savage criticism provoked by Frost's book between March and August by such New Deal liberals as Newton Arvin, Horace Gregory, Richard P. Blackmur, Rolfe Humphries, and Granville Hicks. In August, immediately after Frost's critics had spent their fury against his conservative politics and poetry in *A Further Range*, Hillyer published "A Letter to Robert Frost" in the *Atlantic Monthly*. This, in turn, provoked Granville Hicks to write a satirical parody, "A Letter to Robert Hillyer." To round out his contribution to this battle of the books and politics, Hillyer published *A Letter to Robert Frost and Others* in 1937, consisting of six additional epistolary poems on similar themes. In *The Saturday Review* (January 1, 1938), Bernard De Voto's essay, "The Critics and Robert Frost," brought this literary and political war to a close by answering all of Frost's critics in a prose tribute very similar to Hillyer's defense of his friend.

The opening stanza of Hillyer's poem captures the spirit of their friendship, which was based upon a common love of poetry so strong that it overcomes all of the usual causes which destroy such relationships:

> Our friendship, Robert, firm through twenty years,
> Dares not commend these couplets to your ears:
> How celebrate a thing so rich and strange —
> Two poets whose affection does not change;
> Immune to all the perils Nature sends,
> World war and revolution and kind friends. . . .
>
> Ours is a startling friendship, because art,
> Mother of quarrels who tears friends apart,
> Has bound us ever closer, mind and heart.

Hillyer then recalls the idyllic times and occasions of their meetings in Amherst before the first World War:

> Before the war, among those days that seem
> Bathed in the slanting afterglow of dream,
> Were happy autumn hours when you and I
> Walked down that street still bright in memory.

As so many of Frost's friends were to note over many years, he records that sometimes they would "converse beyond the crack of dawn," and that at times he barely was able to return to Harvard after a night of good talk:

> Myself, too sleepy then as now, would run
> To catch the last car back at half-past one.

47

In retrospect, Hillyer compares their past differences in age and status with their present relationship, two decades later:

> I was a boy apprenticed to my rhymes,
> Your fame already rose above our times,
> Your shadow walking tall, my shorter gait,—
> Both taller now, the difference as great.

From his "many conversations" with his mentor, Hillyer confesses his indebtedness in having acquired aesthetic principles in his art which twenty years later still move him when he is not consciously aware of them:

> Of wisdom I learned much, an Artist's creed
> Of work the flower, and worldy fame the weed;
> I have forgotten phrases; it remains
> As part of me, it courses in my veins.

Hillyer did indeed acquire from Frost his theory of art and his practical conception of creativity in poetry. Toward the close of his life, twenty-four years after he wrote his poetic tribute, in his book *In Pursuit of Poetry* (1960), Hillyer's indebtedness to Frost is reflected in sixteen examples of techniques or forms of poetry drawn from Frost's poetry and ideas, four of which extend to several pages each. By combining "A Letter to Robert Frost" with other of Hillyer's verses and with his prose statements on Frost in *Some Roots of English Poetry* (1933), and *In Pursuit of Poetry* (1960), it is possible to construct in some detail their basic agreements and disagreements on important subjects.

Both Frost and Hillyer were traditionalists in their religion, politics, conception of society and human nature, and views of art and poetry. Both poets explicitly expressed their faith in God. Their conception of humanity as essentially finite, flawed, and limited in power was qualified by their belief that individuals had a great capacity for positive self-fulfillment and achievements of a high order. Both men were skeptical that changes in society through radical reforms or revolution could do as much good as widespread self-discipline and improvements in individuals. Frost's invitation in "Build Soil" "to a one-man revolution" finds its counterpart in Hillyer's poem, "Variations on a Theme, IV":

> The only active war or revolution
> Each man must fight within his soul.

Their common conservative temperament and convictions about mankind in institutionally organized society led them to believe that history and experience were far more trustworthy guides than abstract reason and ideological speculations in making important social changes through politics. They shared a profound skepticism about self-styled "intellectuals" who constructed rational ideological theories of society that they mistakenly identified with reality and who employed their theories as the basis of radical or revolutionary reforms, which they claimed would result in "progress" or even a Utopian state at the end of historical time. Both men emphatically rejected Marxism. They were also highly skeptical of the Freudian psychological theory of human nature. They held that there are mysteries regarding both spirit and matter, which are better uncovered through traditional beliefs pursued courageously, rather than through speculative reason.

In "A Letter to James B. Munn," Hillyer was of one mind with Frost in his belief that literature and education should not be too separated from daily life:

> Learning and life are too far wretched apart,
> I cannot reconcile, for all my art,
> Studies that go one way and life another,
> Tastes that demoralize, and tests that smother.

Yet since the wisdom of life reaches back centuries in the experience of mankind, both Frost and Hillyer held that the poets of classical antiquity were valuable in contemporary life. In this regard the younger poet praised Frost's classical learning and connected it with the originality and the source of his colloquial realism as manifested in *North of Boston*. In *Some Roots of English Poetry* Hillyer cautioned readers against being "misled by . . . poets who achieve simplicity into thinking that their range of interests is confined to a few themes and a few times from the life around them." He observed that this "may be said of our greatest living American poet, Robert Frost," who "sprang into fame as the exponent of northern New England in his own speech." Hillyer then summarized some of the complex elements in Frost's background that made his technique, forms of expression, and skills as a poet so subtle and deceptively simple:

His first volumes were adversely criticised for their colloquial method. A study of Frost, however, soon convinces us that the deliberate ruggedness of his verse has beneath it a carefully modulated music, and that his pictures of the starker aspects of farm life are by no means merely photographic realism but represent phases in the relations between mankind and nature, and are symbols of man's unremitting strife. It is significant that the poet himself, although he speaks with his own voice so individually, completely withdraws himself from the emotional content of his work. When we seek for the roots which sustain his poetry, we at first find the obvious one, that of New England: yet there is another going back into English literature through the work of George Crabbe, and there is yet another . . . which goes straight back to Greek literature. Frost is an excellent Greek scholar, and the philosophers of Athens have molded his thought.

Hillyer concludes his thesis that the apparent simplicity in Frost's art and in his New England colloquial idiom reaches back through English literature to the Ancient Greeks, in an "unbroken continuity of all good poetry beyond the identification of names and ages," by providing an anecdote from his personal experience:

> I remember that some years ago a student was pleading for the rootless sort of poetry which was in vogue then, and that he cited Robert Frost as an example of a man who had developed through his inborn talent alone without recourse to the past. By good fortune a professor of Greek who formerly had taught Mr. Frost was present, and summoned us into his study. He produced his old records, opened to Frost's name, and there across the page, recitation after recitation, test after test, was an unbroken series of A grades.
>
> (Hillyer, *Some Roots* 15-17)

Hillyer knew not only that Frost was no primitivist but also that he was thoroughly saturated with the literary and philosophical traditions of over twenty centuries of European and American art and thought.

In the light of this understanding of Frost, Hillyer had no qualms in believing with his mentor that true originality in lyrical, narrative, and dramatic poetry was to be found in creating new ways of using old techniques and forms of poetry, and not in innovative experiments that deliberately shattered traditional usage, like those of the Imagists.

Hillyer's pastoral poems and lyrics find their counterpart in Frost's techniques and forms of poetry. Like the older poet, he uses a variety of traditional patterned stanzas; and the phonetic devices in his poems include a more or less strict but flexible use of iambic meter, in rhythms that cut across the meter to produce the tone or mood of a poem, and in functional rhymes. Like Frost, he also wrote some long reflective poems. In addition to his seven epistolary pieces, Hillyer's narrative work includes "The Halt in the Garden," "Prothalamion," "Manorbier," "The Gates of the Compass," and "The Death of Captain Nemo." In all of these poems Hillyer differs very markedly from Frost in his rhetorical diction, which is, of course, a world apart from Frost's colloquial idiom.

Like Frost, Hillyer had very strong reservations about scientific scholarship when applied to the study of poetry. He attacks the pedantry of literary scholars who "dig old garbage from the kitchen midden" in search of esoteric trivial poems of no aesthetic merit, while neglecting the important and enduring works of such poets as Frost. In "A Letter to James B. Munn," he contends ironically that the omission of such misplaced searches by scholarly pedants would result by default in a gain of recognition for Frost:

> Surely our sprite, who over Amherst hovered,
> Would gain if no more poems were discovered.

Hillyer's own very favorable critical judgment of Frost's verse is based upon his perception of its place amidst contemporary poetry, which, he insists, has its roots in the whole tradition of Western classical literature: "Until the publication of Frost's *North of Boston* in 1914 . . . there was a complete lack of contemporary American poetry in the grand tradition" (*In Pursuit* 187). In the phonetic patterns and voice tones in Frost's pastorals and eclogues, particularly in the dialogue of his blank verse, with its frequent extra iambic foot or syllable, Hillyer perceived a close affinity with the tradition of colloquial blank verse established in Elizabethan dramatic verse: "Elizabethan dramatic blank verse established the form in a series of important works which have extended down to our day in much of the work of E. A. Robinson and Robert Frost" (*In Pursuit* 25).

In illustrating various traditional forms of poetry, Hillyer drew heavily for his examples from Frost's work. He quotes Frost's "The Aim Was Song" for a model of the ballad stanza (*In Pursuit* 59-60). "The Tuft of Flowers" is his specimen of the couplet used as an independent stanza (*In Pursuit* 64-65). For an excellent sample of blank verse in a dramatic dialogue Hillyer cites Frost's "West-Running Brook" and "The Death of the Hired Man" (*In Pursuit* 82). His ideal modern sonnet is "The Silken Tent" (*In Pursuit* 113), which he quotes in full. Hillyer contends that the pastoral poems of Frost are "realistic" because the poet prefers for his New England scenes the spirit of George Crabbe's "The Village" to the sentimental account of farm life in Oliver Goldsmith's "The Deserted Village" (*In Pursuit* 146-47). He approved of Frost's admiration for Longfellow as a poet, and provides his own equally favorable estimate: "Longfellow was a good poet and frequently escaped his self-imposed conservatism" (*Some Roots of English Poetry* 6).

In a lengthy discussion of modern poets whose work is "the result of sound self-criticism . . . or of inspiration trained to excellent achievement," Hillyer presents Frost as his best example of such poets:

The pattern of such performance, undeviatingly pursuing its highest aim, was set by our living classic, Robert Frost, from the first poem he ever published to the present. He is still with us, having gone his own way unruffled while so many vogues sprang up around him and vanished. Sturdy, wise, and active, he remains unconfused in times when personal confusion is almost a fad, unafraid in what lesser folk have called an age of anxiety. The effect of his influence is incalculable. Recording people and nature acutely and often humorously, he reawakens and sustains our faith in human destiny and, in particular, the importance of man as a responsible individual. He is the bearer of good tidings, knowing that

> The bearer of evil tidings,
> When he was half-way there,
> Remembered that evil tidings
> Were a dangerous things to bear.

Sorrow is in his poetry as well as joy, love most of all, and a light, satirical scorn for what is too unworthy to be dwelt upon. His most playful sentence may suddenly be discovered to be one of his most serious. When we are with him, at his slightest remark we turn, and find ourselves as in a mountain meadow with all the expanses of the world spread out below us.

We chose our destiny before we were born, he says, and it is our lifework to make the most of it, rebounding from failure to try something else:

> There is our wildest mount, a headless horse,
> And though it runs unbridled off its course,
> And all our blandishments would seem defied,
> We have ideas yet that we haven't tried.

He bids us take a chance on life:

> Have I not walked without an upward look
> Of caution under stars that very well
> Might not have missed me when they shot and fell?
> It was a risk I had to take—and took.

"For me," he says, "the initial delight is in the surprise of remembering something I didn't know I knew." And a poem "begins in delight and ends in wisdom." This is the true quality of his work, and since . . . much of his poetry is a dialogue between Frost and his reader, nothing remains unshared or unexplored between the two.

I have already defined the great poet as the one who gives us the best of himself and his experience of life as he has known it in his time. This is an accurate description of Frost. Were I writing music instead of prose, this paragraph would be a tremendous chorale, a sounding finale, in his honor. As it is, I can only say that Frost towers over every other twentieth-century American poet, our undisputed master beyond time.   (*In Pursuit* 216-18)

Hillyer's intimate knowledge of Frost's theory of poetry and practice as a poet, so evident throughout this sustained critical commentary, makes his view of Frost as the foremost twentieth-century American poet less extravagant than it appears to be, particularly because he regarded music as the supreme form of art.[1]

In his attempt to connect particular poems of Frost with the long-established themes and techniques of past traditions, Hillyer's interpretations sometimes miss the mark. He cites as Frost's treatment of "the theme of *carpe diem*" these lines from "Birches":

> Earth's the right place for love,
> I don't know where it's likely to go better.

But much more than the *carpe diem* theme, these lines really express Frost's skepticism toward the idealized Platonic view of love and transcendent reality. However, Hillyer redeems his error in his subsequent critical comments. He notes that these earth-anchored lines, in their tone, express a melancholy longing for the lost Eden, a homesickness and yearning that can only be replaced by "the gardens of the Hesperides that lie before," which involves a realistic acceptance of life in the present, with all its joys and tragedies. In a still further refinement, he then connects the Edenic theme in Frost with "the transmutation of familiar events and landscapes into symbols of man and his drama on the stage of time. This revelation of the eternal in the familiar is one of the most important aspects of poetry" (*In Pursuit* 6). In perceiving the connection that enables poetry to link the eternal transcendent ideal as spiritual reality with the mundane familiar world of sensory experience, Hillyer comes close to summarizing in practice Frost's belief that poetry attempts to say spirit in terms of matter, or matter in terms of spirit, to achieve the final synthesis (*In Pursuit* 6-7).

In view of how closely Hillyer agrees with Frost's theory of poetry, it is perhaps surprising that so few of his own poems resemble those of his mentor. They frequently share common subjects in the pastoral tradition, and both poets make use of long-established techniques and forms of poetry. But Hillyer's rhetorical diction and general lack of metaphor create a tone that is a world removed from Frost's colloquial mode of expression and richness in imagery.

Perhaps the closest that Hillyer comes to an actual imitation of Frost is in his dramatic dialogue "The Assassination," which in its subject, theme, and dramatic technique closely resembles Frost's "The Lovely Shall Be

Choosers." In Hillyer's lyric the "First Fate" and "Second Fate" correspond in their dialogue with "the Voice" and "the Voices" in Frost's poem. The subject addressed by the two Fates is a stoical man identified as "Hope," whom the two Fates pursue through various stages of his life to his inevitable death. In Frost's lyrical drama the Voice and the Voices aim at the same final end of a lovely woman whose initial choice of love over wealth and honor is doomed beyond her seven joys in life to final tragedy and death. Both Hillyer and Frost share a tragic vision of the human condition on earth. In the trial by existence the theme in both poems is that the Fate which guides and rules each human life determines its final outcome beyond any of the initial free choices taken in pursuit of happiness. In both poems temporality is the mortal enemy of hope or love and determines the final tragedy, which ends in death.

Despite their many similarities regarding poetry and literature in general, and their common religious, social, and political views, some important differences separated the two poets. Hillyer shows very little awareness of the extent and depth of Frost's dualistic conception of reality as both spirit and matter, which provides the whole basis of his complex philosophy. In Hillyer's many comments on his friend, there is no evidence that he perceived Frost's belief that reality consists of an eternal conflict "between God and the Devil, between the rich and the poor . . . and . . . between endless other things in pairs ordained to everlasting opposition."[2] Perhaps the main difference between the two poets was a matter of temperament. Hillyer was very comfortable in his feelings regarding the academic profession and the Harvard environment, in sharp contrast with Frost, who was always ill at ease in, and out of harmony with, every educational institution he served. This fact goes far in explaining the differences in their verse. Although Hillyer recognized that "Robert Frost's poetry seldom departs from the conversational style," and although he believed that "there are two kinds of style, the *rhetorical*, heightened and dignified, and the *conversational*, informal and familiar" (*In Pursuit* 17), his own style was almost wholly rhetorical. This vital disparity in language makes the tone of his poetry vastly different from that of Frost; it also explains why their respective views of particular persons and poets were sometimes so different.

An even more serious divergence between the two poets is found in Hillyer's exalted opinion of Robert Bridges as one of the foremost poets of the twentieth century. He described Bridges's poetry as "calm as the sea and flowing as a river," and praised him as rooted in his native land and culture:

Who knew his source and end, but also knew
The homely country he meandered through.

Bridges's *The Testament of Beauty* was for Hillyer among the ultimate aesthetic conceptions of art and poetry.[3] To Frost the "calm" tone and facile movement of Bridges's poetry was simply dull. From the moment that Frost met the laureate in London in 1913, he was highly skeptical about his "brave theory of rhythm" regarding poetry. On December 15, 1913, he wrote at length about Bridges's theory to his friend John T. Bartlett and expressed his doubt that in English "our syllables are to be treated in verse as having quantities of many shades" (*Selected Letters* 103-104). Frost has made it crystal clear why and how his own theory of language is the antithesis of Bridges's theory:

> He rides two hobbies tandem, his theory that syllables in English have fixed quantity that cannot be disregarded in reading verse, and his theory that with forty or fifty or sixty characters he can capture and hold for all time the sounds of speech. One theory is as bad as the other and I think owing to much the same fallacy. The living part of a poem is the intonation entangled somehow in the syntax and meaning of a sentence. It is only there for those who have heard it previously in conversation. It is not for us in any Greek or Latin poem because our ears have not been filled with the tones of Greek and Roman talk. It is the most volatile and at the same time important part of poetry. It goes and the language becomes a dead language, the poetry dead poetry. . . . When men no longer know the intonation on which we string our words they will fall back on what I may call the absolute length of our syllables which is the length we would give them in passages that meant nothing. . . . English poetry would then be read as Latin poetry is now read and as of course Latin poetry was never read by Romans. Bridges would like it read so now for the sake of scientific exactness. Because our poetry must sometime be as dead as our language must, Bridges would like it treated as if it were dead already.
>
> (Thompson, *Early Years* 443)

Where Hillyer found power in Bridges's understatement and self-restraint, interpreting these traits as classical decorum, Frost considered Bridges's calm and easy flowing metrical lines as signs of a dead language in dead poetry.

Biographers and literary critics of Frost and Hillyer have thus far neglected to do full justice to their long, friendly, and complex relationship. This brief essay has merely touched upon some of the vital details that mark their similarities and differences in their thought and art. What their friendship meant to each poet has yet to be determined. But a remark by Hillyer may provide the key to how a future, complete study of the Frost-Hillyer relationship should be pursued: "Well, as Robert Frost said to me one day about good work that is neglected: 'The books are there. Someone some time will take them down from the shelf'" (*In Pursuit* 185).

NOTES

[1] See Hillyer, "A Letter to James B. Munn," in *A Letter to Robert Frost and Others* 27-28.

[2] Robert Frost, "Introduction" to *Threescore: The Autobiography of Sarah N. Cleghorn* (New York: Arno P, 1980) x.

[3] For Hillyer's frequent praise of Bridges and *The Testament of Beauty*, see *Some Roots of English Poetry*, passim, and *In Pursuit of Poetry* 29, 115, 133, 175-77.

WORKS CITED

Frost, Robert. "Introduction" to *Threescore: The Autobiography of Sarah N. Cleghorn*. New York: Arno P, 1980.

Hillyer, Robert. *A Letter to Robert Frost and Others*. New York: Knopf, 1937.

———. *In Pursuit of Poetry*. New York: McGraw-Hill, 1960.

———. *Some Roots of English Poetry*. Norton, MA: Wheaton College, 1933.

Thompson, Lawrance, ed. *Selected Letters of Robert Frost*. New York: Holt, Rinehart and Winston, 1964.

———. *Robert Frost: The Early Years, 1874-1915*. New York: Holt, Rinehart and Winston, 1966.

Mark Van Doren and Robert Frost

Mordecai Marcus

Mark Van Doren (1894-1972), the distinguished teacher and man of letters, left behind him a large body of writing that included critical studies of Thoreau, Dryden, Shakespeare, and Hawthorne; countless essays and reviews, collected and uncollected; several anthologies; three novels and many collection of stories; several plays; a fine autobiography; and almost 1,000 pages of poetry—including several long narratives—often closely printed. His *Collected Poems, 1922-1938* won a Pulitzer Prize. The published body of his poetry is more than twice as large as Robert Frost's. Since Van Doren displayed great ease and facility in all he wrote, it is not surprising that only a small proportion of his poems are memorable. These, however, include some of the best poetry of his time. From the beginning of his poetic career to reviews of a posthumous collection, Van Doren was described as a follower of Robert Frost, though his friend Allen Tate took the intriguingly variant view that Van Doren showed "a good deal of Robinson, less of Frost, something of Hardy."

In *Robert Frost: The Years of Triumph*, Lawrance Thompson describes Van Doren as a friend of Frost (627) but offers no details about their relationship, nor did Thompson include any Frost-Van Doren correspondence in his edition of Frost's letters. Stanley Burnshaw mentions several occasions on which Van Doren and Frost were present together, mostly birthday celebrations for Frost at which Van Doren sometimes read or spoke, but again we learn nothing about their personal relationship. Van Doren published several reviews of Frost collections, one fine general essay on him, perceptive explications of "Once by the Pacific" and "The Oven Bird," and a literary obituary. Van Doren's *Autobiography* says nothing about a personal relationship but admiringly describes letters he received from Frost and comments briefly on his poetry (169-71). After Van Doren requested Frost's permission to include two poems in his *Anthology of World Poetry*, Frost sent a coy reply implying that it wasn't worth Frost's while to be so slightly represented. When Van Doren increased his request to four poems, Frost granted permission and complimented Van Doren on his sharpness as a reader of character and letters. Later, Frost wrote to praise Van Doren's pastoral narrative *A Winter Diary*, and the two exchanged letters when Frost submitted poems to *The Nation* and begged Van Doren's indulgence in waiting for revisions. In expressing admiration for Hardy and Robinson, Van Doren turns his focus to Frost, praising him for a humor superior to Robinson's, for—he maintains—there is "no poem of Frost's that does not derive dimension from it and the name of that dimension is depth" (169).

The similarities in experience, temperament, and outlook of these two poets are impressive, though they crisscross in a variety of ways. Unlike Frost's, Van Doren's beginnings were rural. He was born and reared on an Illinois farm, where his father was a country doctor who also owned and managed several farms. Thus he grew up surrounded by country things, and this was the kind of environment he returned to when he could. Frost was transplanted from urban California to small-town New England at the age of eleven. At a similar age, Van Doren's family moved from rural Hope, Illinois, to Urbana, the seat of the state University, where Van Doren received his B.A. and M.A. degrees. Van Doren's family was large and affectionate, but his awareness of the human suffering that his physician father witnessed and his general responsiveness to people sensitized him to the scope of human ills. At an early age, Van Doren embarked on doctoral studies at Columbia University and after his graduation joined its English Department, where he remained active until his retirement in 1959. Shortly after his marriage in 1922, Van Doren purchased a farm in rural Cornwall, Connecticut, and spent all of his summers, two sabbatical years, and all of his retirement years there. Van Doren was quite active on his farm and keenly inquisitive and observant of the life of people and nature in northwestern Connecticut. While teaching at Columbia, he occupied a house in downtown Manhattan and was deeply immersed in American intellectual life. Thus Van Doren was exposed to and inspired by representative rural and urban worlds.

Frost's paths parallel Van Doren's in several interesting ways. He, too, spent much of his adult life in rural environments, but he taught for many years at assorted colleges and universities, some of them urban. Frost was never a professionalized teacher, but as teacher and thinker he had a lot in common with Van Doren. Van Doren declined to be a specialist, taking American, English, and world literature as his province. Frost also read and taught literary works from all periods, both on and off the beaten track, sharing with Van Doren a love of Shakespeare, Milton, and Homer. As a teacher, Van Doren treasured the generalizing and ethical power of literature, and gave only passing attention to linguistic niceties; Frost did the same. The two men shared an interest in astronomy, which appears in their poems, and an open-minded and questing religious sensibility. Perhaps most importantly they shared a joy in existence in the face of inexplicable griefs and uncertainties, and a determination to go on to the end, pursuing the light ahead.

A few moderately successful Van Doren poems show the obvious influence of Frost. Among his early poems, "Former Barn Lot" presents in three small quatrains a typical Frostian scene with an attempt at implied generalization. Here is the familiar rural dwelling returned to raw nature; people and farm animals are gone and only a bird sees "Under the wire, / Grass nibbling inward / Like green fire." Frostian pathos and understatement are here and an incisively spare suggestion of nature's vitality as somehow superior to people's, but little of the haunting human figures one sees or senses behind the desolation of Frost's "Ghost House" or "The Need of Being Versed in Country Things." In the same volume, "Dispossessed," a more ambitious poem, is reminiscent of "An Old Man's Winter Night." In eighteen lines of blank verse, Van Doren's speaker enters an unused room in a rural house, dispossessing it from physical decay and from residual insect and animal life, so that it may serve, presumably, as a retreat for writing and study. The poem begins "No hand had come there since the room was closed / To all but what could live with sifting chaff, / And dust, and pale grey webs." The subject is seized with an immediacy that combines naturalness and surprise, and the delicately oppressive atmosphere is captured in simple and convincing language. Phrases like "Whirled dust against the darkened panes" and "No other sound" echo the language and atmosphere of the Frost poem. But Van Doren's speaker is also his protagonist, and the poem proceeds to his quiet triumph, first over "a length of lining board" that he "pulled / Loose from the timbers," and then over insects and mice, these treated with something of the patronizing tenderness of Frost's "White-Tailed Hornet" and Hardy's "An August Midnight." But Van Doren's verse and sentiment falter at the end. His speaker tells us that he never returned to this room but offers no explanation for this strange withdrawal. Furthermore, his conclusion seems an additional non-sequitur: "For all I know the dust is quieter now / Than ever it was; with only the bright-black eyes / Of motionless mice on a beam to say if it is." The attempt to enter the world of dust and mice needs a more emphatic rhythm or a sharper twist away from or back to the main substance of the poem—the kind of conclusion that Frost achieves with "It's thus he does it of a winter's night." Van Doren's poem shows a fine but offhand talent.

Another conspicuously Frostian poems is "Ambush," which features a night-walker speaking in a solid block of iambic couplets, frequently run-over. He describes his walk among darkened houses whose inhabitants seem to pay no attention to him until he sees into a house where "two ancient women sat, / Motionless, their feet upon a mat." These women, he knows, are watching him silently but intently, and as he proceeds, his concluding thoughts are of "Darkness, and a path before a den, / And silent spiders watching men." The poem is a sort of inversion of Frost's "Good Hours," and were it not that "Acquainted with the Night" was first collected the year after "Ambush" appeared, one would suspect a direct influence from it. Still, the connection between a rural atmosphere with initially innocent people and an indwelling sinister possibility that may be more the product of the speaker's state of mind than of the world is reminiscent of Frost. "Ambush" is weakened by sentimental irrelevancies as in "Three happy puppies played about a pool / Until a boy behind them pushed them in," and as in "Dispossessed" by a failure to make the conclusion either sufficiently surprising or deftly linked to what precedes it. This is far from Van Doren's weakest work, but it seems artificially composed rather than designed according to a powerful succession of feelings.

Turning to Van Doren's most accomplished poems, one discovers in them a spirit resembling Frost's but fewer specific treatments and situations like his. Frost allowed his imagination to range freely across history and geography, but only a few of his poems are derived from books, and these are rarely among his best. Van Doren's brilliant "The Distant Runners" begins with an anonymous epigraph about six great horses that the men of the explorer De Soto set free after his death. Van Doren's picture of these magnificent creatures moving gloriously across the ancient plains is a paean to their freedom and a lament for the disappearance of the lyric quality their lives suggest. Stanza after stanza works variations on a contrast between the dead of history and the spiritual death of modern people living in a world devoid of those creatures' splendid freedom. The feet of the horses echo through all of the stanzas, and the sounds they make contrast to a present-day spiritual silence. Van Doren's speaker yearns for that lost world, concluding:

> If I were there to bend and look,
> The sky would know them as they sped
> And turn to see. But I am here
> And they are far, and time is old.
> Within my dream the grass is cold;
> The legs are locked; the sky is dead.

Here, as throughout the poem, the language is fluid but spare; the pulsing rhythms echo both the movement of the horses and the speaker's mental pursuit of them. The poem is Frostian in its pursuit of a lost paradise the speaker wishes to imaginatively recreate but has to acknowledge as out of his reach. The dead sky at the end contrasts with Frost's recurrent hope of some revelation from the stars but bears some resemblance to his slightly sarcastic desperation, in a poem like "Choose Something Like a Star," though it was published long after "The Distant Runners." In "The Distant Runners" Van Doren has more firmly closed down spiritual paths between nature and people than Frost does, but in his work as a whole, like Frost, he keeps them open.

"This Amber Sunstream," Van Doren's most famous poem, was collected in 1935, late enough for it to bear the mark of much of Frost's work, but it is an extraordinarily individual work. The figure in it sits in a room with one hour of daylight left, brooding delicately on the fact of mortality which is made tangible by the flow of the late afternoon sunstream pouring through the room. This sunstream merges with human consciousness of it, so that the two are somehow one. The personified sunstream seems to do as much feeling as the person who shares the room with it. One recalls Frost hesitating outside of woods whose darkness he must resist, but one thinks even more of the figure in "An Old Man's Winter Night," so wrapped up in his thoughts that he has grown unaware of the world that isolates him and that almost dissolves around him. But the strongest touch of Frost here may be the poem's marvelous control of prosody, approaching what Frost called "the sound of sense," combining the worlds of contemplation and of sense impressions. The second stanza illustrates these qualities:

> No living man may know it till this hour,
> When the clear sunstream, thickening to amber,
> Moves like a sea, and the sunk hulls of houses
> Let it come slowly through, as divers clamber,
> Feeling for gold. So not into this room
> Peer the large eyes, unopen to their doom.

The word "living" thrusts free from the iambic pattern to express a yearning for that life threatened by the demise of light. The next line is as dense and smooth, yet it features three metrical variations that create a sound of sense. The first foot is reversed, creating a slight hesitancy. The spondaic second foot emphasizes the density of the light, giving the repeated "sunstream" a special salience. Then, though the three-syllable "thickening" fits the iambic pattern, the combined density of the word and the clicking syllable in its middle make it stand by itself and suggest the consistency of a syrup whose sweetness and tone-color are reinforced by "amber." The stanza continues with similar prosodic skill: the third line begins with a reversed foot, and "sunk hills" forms a spondee whose weight echoes its sense. In the fourth line one feels something of the distant ships of Frost's "Neither Far Out Nor In Deep" and "Sand Dunes" brought inside the world of contemplation. Like Frost's old man, the figure here is nodding off to sleep, and though the tomb named at the end suggests universal fatality, the speaker's voice remains unflinching. In his own way, Van Doren magnificently stands up to his own desert places. The poem concludes with a calm and determined stoicism: "No living man in any western room / But sits at amber sunset round a tomb," where Van Doren's acceptance of fatality has its individual flavor, different from the equally calm stoicism at the end of Frost's great sunset poem "Acceptance": "Let the night be too dark for me to see / Into the future. Let what will be, be."

Comparison of "This Amber Sunstream" and "Acceptance" shows how Van Doren often merges the inner and the outer worlds in a manner less pictorial than Frost's. Frost begins more on the outside and then finds an inner depth within the physical world. Van Doren's world of contemplation begins more on the inside and pulls the outside world into it. This occurs in the very beautiful "Young Woman at a Window," where one hears the voices of both Robinson and Frost. The poem is a ritual of praise for a young woman seen leaning from her window toward darkness and wind which come to symbolize the great unknowns of experience that she faces courageously. As the speaker contemplates her, she seems to dissolve into the "wind-and-water song" outside. She becomes a ghost figure like the young people in several poems from *A Boy's Will*, like the speaker of the later "Bereft," and like several Frost speakers who trudge through woods or wilderness. Van Doren maintains more distance from his character than does Frost and expresses a more direct admiration. The note of persistence here has much of the general affirmation of "No Faith," a reliance on animal faith and praise of it. It also shows an ambiguous yielding to the darkness that may be more reminiscent of Robinson than of Frost, especially in the beautiful concluding lines: "But still the current of the night / Comes with its foaming on and on; / Pours round the sill; dissolves the hands; / And still the dreamless body stands." This balance between seeing the universe as a possible vacuum and the assertion of a deep animal faith also appears in "Axle Song," where the wonder of the speaking voice, pained and baffled by the very fact of existence, accepts things as they are: "So growled the earth's revolving heap / And will forever," lines one might imagine having been written by Robert Frost or Archibald Macleish.

Among Van Doren's finest poems are two, one fairly early and one rather late, that echo Frost's idioms as well as his temperament. These are "Autonomous" and "Wish for the World." In "Autonomous" the movement of the verse and some of the imagery are Frostian. The poem is a satirical portrait of someone who "thinks he made himself, this happy man." The poem proceeds to portray and deride a solipsist who thinks that he created everything that happened to him. The language is condensed, and the witty rhymes echo the boastful sense of complete self-determination by the "autonomous" man, as in "From out the mist of women he contrived / The stepping forth of one whom then he wived," where the rhyme and word-choice of "contrived" expose the boastfulness and artificiality of the self-congratulation. In subsequent lines, the idiom of Frost's "The Onset" is put to strikingly different uses: "The maple where it stands is proof of seed. / He knows it and can measure by its need, / Among so many neighbors, a trunk's tallness; / And by its shade the aftercomer's smallness, / Dwarf to its sire." Van Doren places his protagonist in a Frostian milieu only to have him sense his superiority to it rather than to measure its graciousness and fortuitous promises. The poem ends with Frostian language: "But he is not a tree; / And thinks that he was present in the dark / When skin was chosen over root and bark," a passage strongly reminiscent of the idiom of "Leaves Compared to Flowers," but used to show pretensions rather than humility and grief.

In "Wish for the World," published in 1960, Van Doren may have written his most Frostian poem, for here both the manner and the stance are strongly reminiscent of the master. In twelve lines, forming six four-foot couplets, Van Doren expresses his determined delight in having the world just as it is, conscious that the strength required by such acceptance is the chief source of reward and that any ideal world must exist only beyond this earth. Here are strong echoes of Frost poems extending from "The Trial by Existence" through "Birches" and on to both the Masques. The poem begins with a remarkably Frostian condensation, combining challenge and determination: "Wish for the world that it will never change, / Even if terrible, to total strange." The speaker is prepared for terrible things to happen but implies that if they are like what he has known they will be bearable. He goes on: "Even if good, may there be no excess / Beyond this power to think of more, of less," in which he affirms the necessity of evils against which to measure and exert goodness. He proceeds to say that the nature of heaven and hell can be known only from a perspective beyond the earthly. But this earth remains "its dear self: the single place / Than which all others have exacter grace, / And yet it is the measure," suggesting that we will recognize the ultimates of evil and good only by our struggle here, a struggle that makes us what we are. The poem concludes: "Be it thus / Forever, little world that lengthens us," in which "lengthens" wittily refers to spiritual growth as the outcome of suffering. Van Doren did not share Frost's conservative political stance, but here he affirms that he will not lack for pains to keep him awake, and he rejoices—as Frost often does—in the outcome.

A solid handful of Van Doren's poems, I believe, will persist, and a sense of their kinship with Frost's work can add to our love of them and to our feeling for the distinctive personality that produced them. To say of a minor twentieth-century poet that his best work shows something of Frost, Hardy, and Robinson is high praise, and though he is a minor poet, calling him such in face of "This Amber Sunstream," "The Distant Runners," and "Young Woman at a Window" seems a little impertinent. One regrets that Van Doren could not maintain a consistency of success approaching Frost's, but his better and his best poems, as well as his accomplishments as a person, convey the sense of a life unusually well lived and of choices made with deliberation and wisdom.

WORKS CITED

Burnshaw, Stanley. *Robert Frost Himself.* New York: George Braziller, 1986.

Frost, Robert. *The Poetry of Robert Frost.* Ed. Edward Connery Lathem. New York: Holt, Rinehart and Winston, 1969.

Thompson, Lawrance. *Robert Frost: The Years of Triumph.* New York: Holt, Rinehart and Winston, 1970.

Van Doren, Mark. *The Autobiography of Mark Van Doren.* New York: Harcourt, Brace, 1958.

———. *Collected and New Poems, 1924-1963.* New York: Hill and Wang, 1963.

Robert Frost, James Dickey, and the Lure of Non-Human Otherness

Donald J. Greiner

"Frost furnished the figure of the poet in American life who can speak plainly and deeply at the same time."

—James Dickey

Initiated readers of twentieth-century American literature are not likely to think of Robert Frost and James Dickey together. Although the two poets are among the most widely honored writers of their respective eras, Frost's stately traditional forms and modernist evocation of fear seem foreign to Dickey's experiments with the verse line and ecstatic excursions into life's various experiences. Yet both poets have an unusual affinity with nature, an ability to look, to *see* something in the landscape besides the merely human.

Dickey has expressed his opinions of Frost in two relatively little-known publications: an essay-review of the Frost biography[1] and an interview that he gave for the Frost centennial.[2] Frost is clearly one of the lions in the path. In this essay I should like first to discuss Dickey's assessment of Frost and then to suggest that Dickey responds to Frost's influence by reacting against it. In so doing, Dickey, who came to poetry when the shadow of Frost, Pound, and Eliot loomed large, both defines his differences from his modernist predecessors and identifies his own voice in the long echo of American poetry.

I

"Beloved" is a term to be mistrusted, especially when applied to poets, because poets are usually beloved for only a few of the right reasons and for many of the wrong ones. "Beloved" poets say what we want to hear, or corroborate our self image, or pronounce "sagely" on matters that seem important at the time. "Robert Frost has been long admired for all these things, and is consequently one of the most misread writers in the whole of American literature" (*Byzantium* 200).

Dickey made these statements only a few years after Frost's death in 1963. Aware of the burgeoning tension between the recently published first volume of Lawrance Thompson's "official" biography of Frost and the tenacity of what Dickey calls "The Frost Story," Dickey concedes that for most people Frost is "unassailable, a national treasure, a remnant of the frontier and the Thoreauistic virtues of shrewd Yankeedom": the hero, in short, of American self-reliance that we feel guilty of betraying every time we eat a fast-food dinner or use a computer (200-201). "The Frost Story" begs for a Hollywood production because it evokes, says Dickey, dream, nostalgia, and Frost's "way of reducing all generalities to local fact so that they become not only understandable but controllable" (201).

A successful writer of film scripts, Dickey explains the mythologizing of The Frost Story by suggesting how Hollywood could film The Legend, moving from Frost's years abroad as "a kind of literary Ben Franklin in Georgian England" to the climax of "the Ultimate Reading, the Kennedy Inaugural" (201-202). Basking in the glow of the Frost myth, one can shiver from tingles along the spine and leave the movie theater fully convinced that Frost represents all that is fine, strong, and enduring about America.

The point, of course, is that the American public is as responsible for the lie of the Frost myth as the poet himself, and perhaps more so. To shift focus, therefore, from The Frost Story to the first volume of Thompson's biography is to experience the routing of one's prior assumptions, for, as Dickey writes, Thompson exposes Frost when the poet was not beloved, when he was, indeed, "a fanatically selfish, egocentric, and at times dangerous man; was, from the evidence, one of the least lovable figures in American literature" (203). The conflict between The Frost Story and The Real Frost affects Frost criticism even today, more than three decades after the poet's death, just as Dickey surmised that it would.

Yet for all the lies, all the deception, all the attractiveness of the persona, Frost at "his most rhythmical and cryptic" was, in Dickey's words, a remarkable writer, largely because of his "individualizing and localizing way of getting generalities to reveal themselves—original sin, universal Design, love, death, fate, large meanings of all kinds" (207). And he was remarkable also because of the "technical triumph" of his poetic voice, his creation of "a particular kind of poetry-speaking voice" (208).

Several years after publishing his essay on The Frost Story, Dickey agreed to an interview about Frost as part of the nationwide recognition of the Frost centennial in 1974. Here, with the opportunity of stressing that "The Story" does not finally matter but the poetry does, Dickey celebrates once again Frost's voice, "the plainness and the colloquialism of the language" ("Conversation" 51). He admits the difficulty of dividing Frost the public personality from Frost the artist who "wrote some very *marvelous* poems," but Dickey returns again and again to the sound of Frost's poetry, to Frost's ability "to say the most amazing things without seeming to raise his voice," to the achievement of what Dickey terms "the plain-speaking guy" (53, 54, 56). Yet lurking both in the background of the poems and at the heart of the voice is fear, the metaphysical darkness and terror that Frost, like most modernists, acknowledged and faced. The voice gives the lie to the folksy manner, exposes the truth behind the "cracker-barrel philosophizing," and confirms Frost as a sharp-eyed observer who saw the gulf between the human endeavor and the non-human other (59).

II

This gulf—chasm, barrier, wall—is a key to the Frost-Dickey relationship. Students of modernism know that from 1915 to about 1960 Frost was often linked with Wordsworth and Emerson instead of Pound and Eliot because of his concern with nature. Despite his untraditional use of such traditional poetic staples as woods, flowers, and streams, he was read as a conventional nature poet who had failed, unlike his great peers, to break with outmoded, nineteenth-century concepts of nature. One had only to read his remarks about Wordsworth, Thoreau, and Emerson—or, better yet, *read* his poetry—to know that such was not the case, but the fact remains that in the eyes of many astute commentators Frost's subject matter disqualified him from the role of modern poet.[3]

Joseph Warren Beach discussed the complexity of the issue in his comprehensive *The Concept of Nature in Nineteenth-Century English Poetry*,[4] but Beach insisted—his book was published in 1936—that the modern literary mind was no longer willing to grapple with the venerable question of humanity's place in nature. Beach believed that in twentieth-century poetry descriptions of natural beauty had been divorced from concepts of universal nature, with the result that the earth and stars were either regarded as scenery or studied as objects. And more: Beach argued that modern poets refused to laud nature's inherent order or to point to it as evidence that humanity's fate develops rationally.

The result of such an understanding of nature poetry was inevitable. If poetry failed to fit Beach's definition, it was dismissed as perhaps good poetry but not good nature poetry. According to Beach, poems that lack a philosophical framework, no matter the intensity of their concern with nature, cannot qualify as nature poetry. In such a scheme, even Frost might be relegated to the scrapheap as surely an important poet but denied, on the one hand, the company of the modernists because he writes about objects in nature and, on the other hand, the brotherhood of nature poets because he does not write philosophically about nature.

Beach's analysis is penetrating, but it also illustrates the dilemma he experienced when faced with a poet like Frost (not to mention Dickey) who was not allowed to be a modernist because he wrote about nature, yet could not be a nature poet because he was not philosophical. Although Frost understands that nature can be a catalyst to get the mind, emotions, and imagination working, he also depicts nature as non-human otherness. He is not only post-Emersonian but also post-Darwinian in his rendering of natural forces. The gulf between humanity and nature is so wide in Frost's major poetry that the separation of the two seems eternal.

Even in the minor "Two Look at Two" which, at first reading, seems to be a sentimental, nineteenth-century account of people and animals silently communicating, Frost stresses the "barbed-wire binding" and the washed-out path between the lovers and the deer. Humans cannot "touch" nature. They can only interpret it. As Frost shows in "The Most of It," another poem about a man and a deer, the interpretation is likely to be wrong. The natural world in Frost is at worst threatening and at best impersonal, unable to express kinship and unwilling to return love. One need only read "Neither Out Far Nor In Deep" and "Design" to understand that while Frost may not be "philosophical" he is a nature poet with a modernist sensibility.

Dickey lauds the voice that Frost developed to probe this peculiarly twentieth-century gulf, but he does not agree with Frost's sense of the inviolability of the separation. Known as a poet of risk, as a man eager to confront what he calls "perpetual possibility," Dickey opens himself to nature and takes chances where he cannot predict the outcome.[5] Indeed, his earlier collections[6] are primarily life-affirming *because* they reject Frost's gulf and investigate instead the mystical connection between humanity and non-human otherness. The sheer physical elements of experience-in-nature fascinate Dickey, and when he discusses poetry in general he often stresses his own visceral response to the way he writes rather than Pound's, or Eliot's, or Auden's—or Frost's—intellectual point of view. Frost's influence on Dickey is largely a matter of Dickey's reaction against Frost's and the modernists' "indoorness": "I slowly worked away from the extremely allusive kind of poetry I had been trying to write, doubtless very much under the influence, at several removes, of Pound and Eliot."[7]

Thus Dickey questions the modernists' position that the poet master the "tradition," a concept memorably expressed in Eliot's "Tradition and the Individual Talent" (1919), and he urges instead that the poet plunge into the non-human world: "In the eternal battle between life and poetry or life and art, I'll take life. And if poetry were not a kind of means, in my case, of intensifying experience and of giving a kind of personal value to it I would not have any interest in it whatever."[8] One thinks here of such astonishing poems as "The Other,"[9] in which the poet meets the dead in a "time-stricken forest"; "A Dog Sleeping on My Feet," in which the poet becomes a dog "sent after the flying fox"; and "Springer Mountain," in which the poet steps "out of my shadow" to run with—and become—the deer.

No Frostian barbed-wire binding or washed-out path or stone wall here: Dickey leaps over the chasm and merges with nature, if only for the moment. H. L. Weatherly calls this process in Dickey's poetry "the way of exchange," and he has in mind the "mysterious process of exchange between a man and his opposites."[10] Had Dickey maintained the modernists' intellectual contemplation of nature, had he, in effect, remained on his side of the wall, he might have assented to Frost's sense of fear and uncertainty in the face of nature's inexorable processes. But he does not remain there. The woods *are* lovely, dark, and deep, yet unlike Frost's wary traveler, Dickey ignores the clearing and rushes into the trees: "The relationship of the human being to the great natural cycles of birth and death, the seasons, the growing up of plants and the dying of the leaves, the springing up of other plants out of the dead leaves, the generations of animals and of men, all on the heraldic wheel of existence, is very beautiful to me."[11]

The goal of Dickey's "exchange," of his embrace of the non-human life force, is not merely to see from a different perspective but to achieve a unified vision of life that is a composite of both the human and the other. Intellectual contemplation by itself will not do. Dickey's rejection of Frost's gulf can be joyous because it offers a vital response to experience that the poet would have missed had he remained within his own range of vision, but the rejection is also dangerous because to take Dickey's position seriously is to risk stepping too far outside the self. In the great poem "The Firebombing," for example, the only way the aging pilot can experience the horror of the burned children is to die. Guilt can prevent the poet-figure from making the life-sustaining connection between self and other, but, unlike Frost, Dickey does not accept the walled-off safety of "promises to keep" in the village as a natural condition of being human. Life, in all the senses of the word, is to be found in the snow-smothered woods—no matter how dark, how deep, how terrifying.

The irony is that Dickey, writing in the second half of the twentieth century, may be closer to Joseph Warren Beach's concept of the nineteenth-century nature poet than Frost, who wrote in the first half of this century. Yet such splitting of hairs is finally irrelevant. Like Frost with "The Frost Story," Dickey, too, has cultivated a public persona as a poet larger than life. But unlike his predecessor, he is not absorbed by his own myth. Admiring Frost's great achievement, especially his poetic voice, Dickey concedes influence by reacting against it.

NOTES

[1] James Dickey, *Babel to Byzantium: Poets and Poetry Now* (New York: Farrar, Straus & Giroux, 1968) 200-209.

[2] Donald J. Greiner, "'That Plain Speaking Guy': A Conversation with James Dickey on Robert Frost," *Frost: Centennial Essays*, Vol. 1, ed. Jac L. Tharpe (Jackson: UP of Mississippi, 1974) 51-59.

[3] Robert Frost, "A Tribute to Wordsworth," *Cornell Library Journal* 11 (Spring 1970) 76-99; "Thoreau's *Walden*," *The Listener*, 26 Aug. 1954: 319-20; "On Emerson," *Daedalus* 88 (Fall 1959) 712-18.

[4] (New York: Macmillan, 1936) especially 547-59.

[5] See, for example, Carolyn Kizer and James Boatwright, "A Conversation with James Dickey," *James Dickey: The Expansive Imagination*, ed. Richard J. Calhoun (Deland, FL: Everett/Edwards, 1973) 1-33.

[6] *Into the Stone* (1960), *Drowning with Others* (1962), *Helmets* (1964).

[7] James Dickey, *Self-Interviews* (New York: Doubleday, 1970) 47.

[8] Kizer and Boatwright 19.

[9] See Harold Bloom, "From 'The Other' through *The Early Motion*," *Contemporary Poets*, ed. Bloom (New York: Chelsea House, 1986) 127-42.

[10] H. L. Weatherby, "The Way of Exchange in James Dickey's Poetry," *Sewanee Review* 74 (Summer 1966) 669-80.

[11] Dickey, *Self-Interviews* 68.

Narrowing Our "Soul-From-Soul Abyss": Inward Journeys of Robert Frost, Richard Wilbur, and William Jay Smith

Dorothy Judd Hall

> Far as we aim our signs to reach,
> Far as we often make them reach,
> Across the soul-from-soul abyss,
> There is an aeon-limit set
> Beyond which they are doomed to miss.
>
> —Robert Frost, "A Missive Missile"

"Make a dip for depth," Robert Frost beseeched a group of graduate students in English gathered at Bread Loaf, Vermont, to hear him "say" his poems one summer evening in the early sixties. "Make a dip for depth and take your emotions with you!" Frost was nearing the end of a lifetime spent delving into the depths of self, of nature, and even of God. The poetic "signs" he aimed "Across the soul-from-soul abyss" shine out like shooting stars against the metaphysical darkness of our age.

Following Frost's *directive* to narrow the spiritual gap that separates us, both Richard Wilbur and William Jay Smith have launched their own metaphoric salvos into dim reaches of consciousness and over wide ranges of reality. Each has written a poetic tribute memorializing the perceptible loyalty that still extends northward from the Berkshires, where Wilbur and Smith now live, to that log cabin in the Green Mountains where Frost once pushed back dark woods to make a spiritual clearing.[1]

At the outset of his poetic career—in "Into Mine Own" (*A Boy's Will* 1913)—Frost embarked on an inward journey. His gloss to the poem read: "The youth is persuaded that he will be rather more than less himself for having forsworn the world." "The youth" resolves (in the gloss to "Revelation") "to become intelligible, at least to himself, since there is no help else." Nearly fifty years later, in the final poem of his last book, he "shoulder[s] axe" and moves "Against the trees." He leaves behind "shadowy tracks"—the imprint of an extended spiritual pilgrimage. No longer a youth, he had touched depths of darkness and seen glimpses of

71

light, and his poems form a pattern of clarification that reaches from the dark woods of "Into My Own," through the burnt-out landscape of "Directive," the major poem of his mature years, to the "tinted snow" in his last poem. In the end he came "home," fulfilling the prophecy in "Into My Own": "They would not find me changed from him they knew— / Only more sure of all I thought was true."

For Frost, artistic talent was a radical mystery whose source is buried deep in the primordial nexus of language and being—hidden in the conjunction of word and world:

> No one given to looking under-ground in spring can have failed to notice how a bean starts its growth from the seed. Now the manner of a poet's germination is less like that of a bean in the ground than of a waterspout at sea. He has to begin as a cloud of all the other poets he ever read. That can't be helped. And first the cloud reaches down toward the water from above and then the water reaches up toward the cloud from below and finally cloud and water join together to roll as one pillar between heaven and earth. The base of water he picks up from below is of course all the life he ever lived outside of books.[2]

While Wilbur and Smith, like Frost himself, made a living at college teaching, they write of life both *in* and *out* of books. The poems of all three, arising from "love"—in Wilbur's phrase—"for the things of this world," chart the course of a hidden stream that flows toward an "Otherness" located simultaneously *within* and *beyond* the self. The deeply spiritual nature of that stream is often obscured—in Wilbur by decorum, in Smith by humor, and in Frost by what I have elsewhere spoken of as "reserve."[3] Nevertheless, it is the underlying current in their art. In Wilbur's "The Mind-Reader" we dip deep into its waters and ponder "The mind of God." In Smith's "Journey to the Interior" the stream goes underground into the dark recesses of his Choctaw Indian heritage. And in Frost's major poem, "Directive," we return to its source, to the spring of creativity and spiritual wholeness. Though differences in temperament and cultural heritage mark the individuality of each, the vision of all three is directed toward that invisible realm which Simone Weil (in another context) calls "a point of eternity in the soul."

Ralph Waldo Emerson, Frost's own spiritual forebear, once noted in his *Journals*: "Blessed is the day when the youth discovers that Within and Above are synonyms."[4] Emerson's term "Above" calls for re-examination. Through the ages the notion of "transcendence" has been pictured, in Western imagination, as relative to our presumed human location "down on Earth" in the cosmic scheme. *Cosmological* shifts—from Ptolemaic to Copernican, to post-Newtonian patterns—have occasioned *ontological*

shifts, changes in world-view. The "no-bound" universe of modernity calls into question former categories of "transcendence." That realm "Above" toward which medieval cathedrals pointed their spires is no longer cosmologically viable; and, as we shall see in the case of Smith, it must be further qualified. For my purposes here, "Beyond" might serve better than "Above." The interiority of Frost, as of Wilbur and Smith, resembles a Möbius strip—circling back toward its starting point yet somehow turned upon itself—rather than a purely inward vector. In a major poem of each, the exploration into consciousness ultimately leads beyond the ego-self into a wider awareness of reality, even of the divine.

Frost's "Directive"

In his essay "The Constant Symbol" Frost asserts his belief in an invisible connection between the shape of poetic language and the shape of truth—a *figura* of meaning which the poet wrests from the raw material of living: "Unto these forms did I commend the spirit. . . . Every poem is an epitome of the great predicament; a figure of the will braving alien entanglements."[5] For Frost, "the spirit" binds poetry to its hidden origin, which is *alpha* and *omega* of the poetic journey in "Directive":

> Your destination and your destiny's
> A brook that was the water of the house,
> Cold as a spring as yet so near its source,
> Too lofty and original to rage.

The healing/wholeness reached in this quintessential poem of interiority reflects Frost's own emergence from an extensive period of spiritual darkness. The poem was written in the aftermath of nearly unbearable personal loss precipitated by the death of his daughter Marjorie (1934) and his beloved wife Elinor (1938) and by the suicide of his son Carol (1940). Elsewhere, I have called Frost's "Directive" "a sacramental journey into the depths of self, and back through historical and geological ages" for the recovery of "wholeness."[6] And the price of that recovered wholeness is suffering. The arduous trail through vanished time and landmarks ends, remarkably, with a moment of pristine simplicity:

> Here are your waters and your watering place.
> Drink and be whole again beyond confusion.

73

Richard Wilbur and "The Mind of God"

It is probably safe to think of Wilbur, an avowed Episcopalian, as somewhat more orthodox in religious belief than the "Old-Testament Christian"[7] who had ranged far afield before "put[ting] a sign up *closed* to all but me" ("Directive"). Yet the Frost of *A Masque of Reason*, who delves into the divine mystery of human suffering, is a kindred spirit to the poet who wrote "The Mind-Reader." Frost's journey had been motivated by "a lover's quarrel with the world" ("The Lesson for Today"). Similarly, Wilbur's was impelled by love. Speaking of his poem, "Love Calls Us to the Things of This World," Wilbur once told Sigmund Koch and Rosanna Warren (Robert Penn Warren's daughter) how the poem grew spontaneously from actual experience—his awakening to the splendor of breezy lines of laundry outside his window one morning in Rome "in 1954 or '55":[8]

> The eyes open to a cry of pulleys,
> And spirited from sleep, the astounded soul
> Hangs for a moment bodiless and simple
> As false dawn.
>   Outside the open window
> The morning air is all awash with angels.

Whenever Wilbur spiritually transforms the ordinary world—as in his ecstatic Italian laundryscape—he is writing out of a poetic center that he and Frost share. Both attend to that sacred mystery at the core of all physical reality. Frost's "All Revelations" (first titled "Geode" in *The Yale Review*, Spring 1938), records the "mental thrust" of human intelligence into the universe. The image of the geode (a rock crystal) turns up also in Wilbur's "Icarium Mare." In his discussion of this poem Bruce Michelson admires the "inspired image of 'The saint's geodic skull'": "Not too many lay people, and I suspect few poets, have looked hard at a geode, considered the rounded, dull, exceptionally skull-like exterior shape, and then cracked it open to find dazzling crystal formations hid within."[9] I wonder if Michelson may have overlooked the central metaphor in Frost's "All Revelation"—and the *earlier* title of that poem! The geode image is a clear link between Wilbur and Frost, but subtler connections are implicit in Wilbur's "The Mind-Reader." As Wilbur confided to Sigmund Koch and Rosanna Warren, in that poem he wanted to imagine himself "in the mind of God." Wilbur recounts running into a "mind-reader" back in 1954 on his first night in Rome, outside a local pizzeria. "He proved indeed to be a mind-reader. I used to go back with new friends from time to time to see how much [meeting such a person] shocked them. That kept him in my mind for twenty years." (Two decades intervened before the poem itself emerged.) Asked about the true genesis of the poem, Wilbur replied, "I think it was finally something he said to the Dante expert, Charles Singleton: 'You know that I *can do it.*'" Then to Singleton's "grudging 'Yes'" the mind-reader volunteered, "It's no pleasure, you know, to have *a mind that's like a common latrine*":[10]

> The mind is not a landscape, but if it were
> There would in such case be a tilted moon
> Wheeling beyond the wood through which you groped,
> Its fine spokes breaking in the tangled thickets.
> There would be obfuscations, paths which turned
> To dried-up stream-beds, hemlocks which invited
> Through shiny clearings to a groundless shade;
> And yet in a sure stupor you would come
> At once upon dilapidated cairns,
> Abraded moss, and half-healed blazes leading
> To where, around the turning of a fear,
> The lost thing shone.

The passage can be read from a dual perspective. If the mental "landscape" is the *human* mind of the "mind-reader," then we imagine ourselves inside a gifted but imperfect psyche—one whose topography is overrun with too many memories to find rest, except at some rare moment of clarity. If we read the passage from the *divine* perspective, we are reading a map of the actual world as if it were a projection of the mind of God—of a God who, as Van Gogh once said, "botched it" when He sketched the outlines of the world. Such a divine artist might be riddled with regret for His imperfect creation. (Compare Frost's line in "West-Running Brook": "As if regret were in it and were sacred.") The idea, Wilbur recalled—"that it should be a form of suffering to have a mind that's open to the minds of everyone else—that got me going on the poem":

> Sometimes I wonder if the blame is mine,
> If through a sullen fault of the mind's ear
> I miss a resonance in all their fretting.

Wilbur concludes that his overriding intention in "The Mind-Reader" "has less to do with this man's [the mind-reader's] character, than to make through him a failing gesture toward the idea of God's mind—to ask 'What must God's mind be if it can take in everything that we are thinking and still be inviolate?' For me that was, if not the center of the poem, it was the target." The link Wilbur finds between *suffering* and the *mind-of-God* most assuredly connects him to the Frost of *A Masque of Reason*, where human suffering and divine knowledge are brought into juxtaposition, and God belatedly concedes to Job:

> Too long I've owed you this apology
> For the apparently unmeaning sorrow
> You were afflicted with in those old days.

William Jay Smith and the Cosmic Vanishing Point

To grapple with interiority in the vision of William Jay Smith we should probably erase Emerson's "Above" altogether and inscribe "Below," for Smith's roots extend deep into the Native American soil of his Choctaw ancestors. The light in his poetry seems to shine forth from some primordial realm in one dazzling moment of illumination—like the instant when memory retrieves the "tall Fijian" spearing "a giant turtle" ("Fisher King"). (Specifically, of course, that poem grows out of Smith's naval experience in the South Pacific in World War II.)

> So seeing him, I see again at dawn,
> Beyond the shifting boundaries of night,
> His image, from the dark unconscious drawn,
> Come shimmering and powerful to light.

The "Below" from which light emerges in Smith's poetry is the darkness to which all human vision returns—like the primeval mystery I once felt shrouded beneath the earth, as I watched a grey November twilight fade over the burial mounds at Chillicothe, Ohio. Lame Buffalo, an American Indian of the Sioux tribe, has explained that an awareness of

> the presence of the great Spirit throughout the entire cosmic order establishes among [Native Indians] one of the most complete forms of spirituality known to man. The cosmic, human, and divine are present to one another in a way that is unique. . . . The earth is sacred. It is a living entity in which living entities have origin and destiny.[11]

More than two decades ago William Jay Smith's interiority, his vision, was characterized as "lightness."[12] Through the years one can witness his imagination deepen—as in his long meditative poem "The Tin Can"—and finally grow quite dark indeed. In its shadowy intensity his later lyric,

"Journey to the Interior," is truly masterful. Let it mark a final outpost in that terrifying landscape upon which Frost so frequently trespassed before he staked out his final "clearing." In Smith's poem, all roads lead inward. They are, to echo Wallace Stevens, the "be" that is "finale of seem" ("The Emperor of Ice-Cream"). Smith here brings Frost's apparently arbitrary selection of a path—from two that diverge in "The Road Not Taken"—to its logical-illogical conclusion. Frost's poem itself has double meanings: might the branching pattern that presents us with choice—apparently irreversible—look rather different *sub specie aeternitatis*? Perhaps all our choices, in the long run, are mere phantasms. The hidden ambiguities in Frost tangle with the underbrush through which Smith moves in his "Interior."

Earlier, in his poetic tribute, "Robert Frost: The Road Taken," Smith had inverted Frost's title and pressed further into the unmarked terrain that (by implication in "The Road Not Taken") lay ahead:

> The poet stopped on the edge of night,
>   And the road through dark wound on.
> Black trees arose; the wind was still;
> Blind skeletal walls inched over the hill
>   In the mole-gray dawn.

Smith's eulogy to Frost sowed the seed for his later, more autobiographical poem. "Journey to the Interior" is retrospective, looking backward upon all those phantom decisions we imagined we made on "that morning [when both roads] equally lay." But for the *evening* traveller the abrupt fork becomes a mere chimera. Although the roads in Frost's poem part, stretching onward into woods along a (more or less) flat plane, they will inevitably come together, on the curved surface of the earth, like "parallel" great circles. Thus our fancied "choices" vanish as we discover that all roads eventually turn inward. Smith has captured the darker truth hidden in Frost's poem: that all our short-range options grow increasingly illusory the closer we come to the end of our course:

> He has gone into the forest,
> to the wooded mind in wrath;
> he will follow out the nettles
> and the bindweed path.
>
> He is torn by tangled roots,
> he is trapped by mildewed air;
> he will feed on alder shoots
> and on fungi: in despair

he will pursue each dry creek-bed,
each hot white gully's rough raw stone
till heaven opens overhead
a vast jawbone

and trees around grow toothpick-thin
and a deepening dustcloud swirls about
and every road leads on within
and none leads out.

In Smith's memoir, *Army Brat,* he traces his descent from Chief Mo-shulatubbee, Head of the Choctaw Nation—and further back to the prehistoric Mound Indians who inhabited the American Bottomlands between AD 900 and 1300. At the close of his book Smith writes:

Now returning to these American Bottomlands, to the scenes of my boyhood, the heart of my country and the depth of myself, I felt that I had somehow been touched by that ancient fire. . . . That knowledge and the thought that I might be but the smallest part of a great mysterious whole filled me with a strange joy as I moved slowly on into the night, on toward the east from which I had come.[13]

Smith's realization reminds us—as poetic vision in its finest moments so often does—that our veritable ends are hidden in our beginnings. The apparently simple line from Frost conceals that widsom: "They would not find me changed from him they knew." Up at Bread Loaf, Frost once quipped—in an aside on the poem—"Of course, I'm not the same Frost I was when winter came round last year!" And yet he knew, as Wilbur and Smith were to learn, that the profoundest seeking into self reaches *beyond* the self, for

beyond the White Mountains were the green; beyond both were the Rockies, the Sierras, and, in thought, the Andes and the Himalayas—range beyond range even into the realm of government and religion.[14]

And beyond the horizon is that vanishing point where world and time dissolve.

What did Wilbur and Smith learn from Frost? As I have discussed elsewhere, Frost understood "influence" as an "in-flowing" of the creative spirit (Bergson's *élan vital*) through all artists across time.[15] "Influence" therefore is pervasive. But it is also elusive—difficult to assess. In fact, the term may be too weak to convey the powerful impact of Frost's poetic presence upon all of us whose lives he touched—his legacy of courage in the face of adversity.

During the "request" period after a reading, I once asked Frost to "say" his poem "To Earthward," one of my favorites. It ends:

> When stiff and sore and scarred
> I take away my hand
> From leaning on it hard
> In grass and sand,
>
> The hurt is not enough:
> I long for weight and strength
> To feel the earth as rough
> To all my length.

He pretended not to hear me, though I had positioned myself right under his reading stand! Later, "Doc" Cook (Director of the School of English) whispered to me, "Mr. Frost never reads that poem." But Frost's candor earlier that evening still resonates within me: "A poet must lean hard on the facts, so hard sometimes that they hurt."

NOTES

1 I refer to Wilbur's "Seed Leaves: *Homage to R.F.*," in *New and Collected Poems* (New York: Harcourt Brace Jovanovitch, 1988) 129 (other citations from Wilbur are also to this edition); and Smith's "Robert Frost: The Road Taken," in *Collected Poems: 1939-1989* (New York: Charles Scribners' Sons, 1990) 111 (other poems cited are also in this edition). Quotations from Frost's poems are from Edward Connery Lathem, ed., *The Poetry of Robert Frost* (New York: Holt, Rinehart and Winston, 1969); the glosses cited in the following paragraph are found on pages 529, 530.

2 Edward Connery Lathem, ed., *Robert Frost 100* (Boston: David R. Godine, 1974) 73, Sec. 65: "Introduction" to *The Arts Anthology: Dartmouth Verse 1925*.

3 "Reserve in the Art of Robert Frost," *Texas Quarterly* 6 (Summer 1963) 60-67 (published under the name Dorothy Judd).

4 Quoted in Nathan A. Scott, Jr., *Visions of Presence in Modern American Poetry* (Baltimore: Johns Hopkins UP, 1993) 205.

5 Hyde Cox and Edward Connery Lathem, eds., *Selected Prose of Robert Frost* (New York: Holt, Rinehart and Winston, 1966) 24-25.

6 *Robert Frost: Contours of Belief* (Athens, Ohio: Ohio UP, 1983) 107-108.

7 Dorothy Judd Hall, "An Old testament Christian," *Frost: Centennial Essays* 3, ed. Jac L. Tharpe (Jackson: UP of Mississippi, 1978) 316-49.

8 "Richard Wilbur: Work Processes and Craft of the Poet" (copyright September 1987), videotape in the *Studies of Significant American Artists* series founded by Boston University and The Ford Foundation. Sigmund Koch, Professor of Psychology and Philosophy, served as Project Director of the entire series. Videotapes are housed in the Geddes Language Center, College of Liberal Arts, Boston University.

9   *Wilbur's Poetry: Music in a Scattering Time* (Amherst: U of Massachusetts P, 1991) 215.

10 This and Wilbur's other comments on "The Mind-Reader" are from the taped conversation cited in note 8, above.

11 Ewert H. Cousins, *Christ of the 21st Century* (Rockport, Mass.: Element, 1992) 134.

12 Dorothy Judd Hall, "William Jay Smith and the Art of Lightness," *Southern Humanities Review* 3 (Winter 1968) 67-77.

13 *Army Brat: A Memoir* (Brownsville, Or.: Story Line Press, 1991) 219.

14 Robert Frost, *A Further Range* (New York: Henry Holt, 1936), Dedication: "To E[linor] F[rost] for what it may mean to her that . . ."

15 Dorothy Judd Hall, "The Height of Feeling Free: Frost and Bergson," *Texas Quarterly* 19 (Spring 1976) 128-43.

Robert Frost's "The Pasture" and Wendell Berry's "Stay Home": Figures of Love and the Figure the Poem Makes

Edward Ingebretsen, S.J.

My essay builds on Frank Lentricchia's phenomenological insight that any particular landscape is "coherent because the mind of the artist makes it so."[1] A poet's "landscapes"—organized fields of perception and control—are metaphors of artistic coherence, and offer "prospects" of meaning into the verse itself.

Frost remarked once that he was always "arguing" with someone in his poems. Many poets since Frost—I can think of Roethke and Wendell Berry, among others—continue to argue with, clarify, even advance Frost's thinking. Wendell Berry, in particular, most directly confirms Frost's insight into the mutuality of love and poetry. In addition, he closely aligns himself with the spiritual universe of Robert Frost, making his chief theme domesticity (agrarian and human). For Berry, too, life, well-lived in a post-lapsarian world, necessarily includes a spiritual commitment to labor and to the complexities of love. Only by tilling the land does one tell the soul. In "Stay Home," Berry's quiet echo of "The Pasture," he offers a loving tribute to an older poet and mentor, while, at the same time, demonstrating the sometimes profound differences in their poetics and in their art. In this essay I wish to consider briefly Frost's "The Pasture" and then explore some ways in which Berry's "Stay Home" echoes, confirms, and focusses the conjunction of love, labor and the land that is so central to both poets.

"The Pasture"—the invitation to the symbolic topography of Robert Frost—is an important poem. It is erotic in the quiet, uninsistent way characteristic of Frost: its text weaves hunger and desire, inclusion and exclusion, living and dying. It offers, in Gaston Bachelard's expression, the hope of "felicitous space," one closed and private, yet somehow very public. Further, "The Pasture" shows how Frost's poetics consciously employs a rhetoric of intimacy. The figure the poem makes, like love, is a figure of the necessary erotics of the imaginative life. "A Cabin in the

81

Clearing," for instance, best articulates Frost's Miltonian, post-lapsarian Eden, a model congenial to Wendell Berry's conviction that in this world "what we have prepared / to have, we have."[2]

Intimacy, according to Frost, whether personal or poetic, is a matter of making space, making time, and knowing what to do with the spaces you had. Through a series of indirections and displacements, love emerges as Frost's most well-imagined symbolic space. And it is in this respect that Berry most clearly follows Frost's lead. Listen, first, to Frost as he speaks designedly about writing poems: "The figure a poem makes. It begins in delight and ends in wisdom. The figure is the same as for love."[3] Love and poems: the figure of the poem is emblematic of love. The figure of the poem, like the figure of love, exists as a set of tensions between public and private discourse, between authority and invitation, between inclusion and exclusion. The poetic text, like the figure of love, establishes a place of engagement and knowing not accessible to all. Love and poetry are risky, places of danger, Frost would say. Neither is a safe place for the unwary or the faint-hearted.

Frost wrote "The Pasture" as a peace offering for his wife Elinor following a domestic misunderstanding. In 1931 he moved it from its original position in *North of Boston* and placed it as the introductory poem for the volume of his collected works. As an offering of love, and as a poem about symbolic spaces, "The Pasture" also provides a theoretical look at the work of intimacy: making space for, making time for. Frost's metaphor is clear: the figure the poem makes is the figure the man and woman make—and that figure, largely figured, is the pasture itself, a place of cultivation, labor—a place, really, of passionate preference, an expression Frost favored. The erotic here, as everywhere in Frost, invites without insisting. A good companion piece in this regard is the later "Putting in the Seed," in which the poet explores the necessary ways human love entangles with, and enables, other sorts of "harvests."

In "The Pasture," the speaker invites an unnamed other to a walk in the pasture. One assumes that a previous intimacy renders naming unnecessary or superfluous:

> I'm going out to clean the pasture spring;
> I'll only stop to rake the leaves away
> (And wait to watch the water clear, I may):
> I shan't be gone long.—You come too.
>
> I'm going out to fetch the little calf
> That's standing by the mother. It's so young
> It totters when she licks it with her tongue.
> I shan't be gone long.—You come too.[4]

In addition, however, as the poem Frost chose to introduce his poetry, "The Pasture" triangulates in an interesting way, since the reader becomes the "unnamed other" who is invited into a kind of pastureland— that wild place tamed, "worked up to form" by human hands. Frost's small pasture is emblematic of a world where "strongly spent is kept," where men and women must spend themselves in labor, paradoxically, in order to keep themselves human; and that basic relationship between the land and its people is, humanly, the "sweetest dream that labor knows" ("Mowing"). Frost follows the implications of his analogy carefully, as "The Pasture" accrues to itself a complex variety of symbolic meanings. While representing human labor as creating a safe and fertile place, it also suggests a different sort of terrain and a different kind of labor: the reader now participates in the sharing of space and labor in the land of unlikeness, verse.

Thus, as a poem, a verbal construction, "The Pasture" offers a different erotic delight, an invitation to a world of verse, where Frost's turnings and versings on a theme demonstrate the inevitable erotic quality of words, and where love, indeed, is grammar, subject and, finally, motive. Since words go where bodies cannot, they contain and shape human experience. They symbolize what is otherwise only "real" in a manner of speaking. Words give form to the very imagination that they construct. Consequently words become charged with the sacred force of revelation: they uncover, make public, and thus criticize human action. Words are, Frost said, literature: "words that have become deeds."

Wendell Berry's long view of the historicity of human love develops Frost's insight that literature, primarily, is one debt we owe to those who have gone before us. Still, for both poets this merely elaborates the centrality of specific and concrete human instances of domesticity and love. Thus, Berry, like Frost, naturally conflates human love with geographical metaphors—recall, for example, *The Country of Marriage* (1973). Further, if Frost's religious sensibility can be understood as derivatively Miltonian, Berry's organicism and domestic commitment emerge from a fundamentally post-Calvinist cosmology. His volume of Sabbath meditations (*Sabbaths*) serves, really, to explicate the title of his first book of verse—*The Broken Ground* (1964)—and Berry's insight is Frost's. Ground must be broken, labored, worked up, spent. At the same time, Berry's title adds the Calvinistic sense of brokenness that touches the land and all human enterprise. In "Stay Home" Berry's twin ideological commitments—Calvinism and organicism—darken Frost's love poem:

I will wait here in the fields
to see how well the rain
brings on the grass.
In the labor of the fields
longer than a man's life
I am at home. Don't come with me.
You stay home too.

I will be standing in the woods
where the old trees
move only with the wind
and then with gravity.
In the stillness of the trees
I am at home. Don't come with me.
You stay home too. (199)

Frost's half-wild, half-tame area of land—the pasture—is, in Berry's revision, only a distant echo, as the speaker waits first "in the field" and then stands "in the woods." Frost, of course, was no stranger to dark woods—they offer an omnipresent shade to his poetic landscapes, though Frost's woods seem dark less because of natural shadows than because of moral, human ones. It is as if, Frost hints (more darkly than Emerson knew or dared), natural facts reflect our spiritual conditions. Frost's "Desert Places" or "Stopping by Woods on a Snowy Evening" or "The Woodpile," for example, describe bleak terrains, yet one has the sense, as with Berry, that the bleakness and danger are not all in the woods. It is in the people who inhabit the woods. Frost's terrains—the woods and clearings, fields and snow—chart, above all, the darker geographies of the soul—the dangerous places—physical and symbolic, in which people find themselves, and from which they must extricate themselves, not to save their humanity, but first to *find* it.

Berry, of course, agreed with Frost (and the Emersonian tradition in general, so far as it went) that natural facts reflect spiritual conditions, though he differs from Frost in the way he imagines the dark woods. In many of Frost's poems the speaker stands "at the edge" of the woods, taking what security he can in "human things"—human love. Throughout Berry's poetry, however, the dark shadows of Frost's woods are not, in fact, out *there*. More often than not they are in the home itself. Further, in Berry's "Stay Home," one senses that the woods and fields are not, finally, to be brought under the sway of human efforts—that the "labor of the fields" is "longer than a man's life." Indeed, next to Frost's almost sentimental evocation of domesticity and human love, Berry's love poems —like his poems of the land—show a darker side of intimacy. Berry's sense is that love, if it is human, is also a kind of broken ground; human love means separation as well as togetherness, where love is as much a "stay[ing] home," working "apart."

Thoreau taught Frost valuable lessons about the need for being grounded—"located"—as Frost used the word in "A Drumlin Woodchuck." And he was from the very beginning conscious of the land. Frost took the idea for the title *North of Boston* from a real estate sign; of his later volumes, five titles directly refer to the land and its topography, while two or three refer to specific aspects of that land. In this respect, too, Wendell Berry echoes Frost, showing the same sort of geographical consciousness —and even, on occasion, borrowing a Frost title as well (e.g., *Clearing*, 1977). But the reference to Thoreau brings to mind the larger American pastoral tradition in which Frost and Berry define themselves. Questions of the land, its definition, meaning, its problematic domesticity, have been a consistent American tension since *Letters from an American Farmer.* If there is a particular American spirituality, poets and thinkers like Thoreau, Emerson, Frost, Wendell Berry—whether meditating on Walden Pond or the Boston Common or on a farm in Kentucky—show its necessary form. Human presence makes a difference, because it draws a line, whether of word or wall or fence—in any event, something not found in nature. And, in love and in poem, it all depends on how you draw the line, establish the space, create the pasture and keep it clear.

In particular, "making a difference"—energy to make it different— inscribes Berry's expanding metaphor: the land as ground of human endeavor, the symbolic place of human risk: the geography that tells the soul. In the last poem of Berry's *Clearing*, the poet perhaps consciously echoes the last poem in Frost's last book, *In The Clearing* (1962). Both poets, walking, meditate upon their journeys. Frost: in the "afterglow" of the afternoon, "In winter in the woods alone / Against the trees I go." Berry: "I go in under foliage / light with rain-light. . . . The way I go is / marriage to this place, / grace beyond chance, / love's braided dance / covering the world" (268).

One senses here Berry's final backward tribute to the source. In the tradition of Thoreau, Emerson and Frost, Berry could say, as Frost did, all literature begins with geography. It is possible, even probable, that Berry was a better farmer than any of the others. But the land served them all, as an organizing metaphor for the drama of human life, as a way of describing the poetry of love and the love of poetry, and their mutual risks—the dangerous, and so human, places in which we find ourselves. It is while in these places, Frost and Berry would agree, that the words of poetry, to use Frost's expression, provide, occasionally, "a way out," a "momentary stay."

Though he might have failed as a farmer, symbolically Frost never lost his fondness for husbandry. Culture—here used in its root sense—always enlivened his imagination. The care for place—as in "to care for" and "to care about"—is central to "The Pasture" and to Frost's verse in general. His decision to let "The Pasture" serve as "introduction" to subsequent volumes of collected poems marks his way of returning to the land—not as a real farmer, but more importantly as a symbolic one, to a symbolic place. He is one who figured and crafted, one who tilled the land by telling the soul. Like Thoreau, Frost found physical movement aptly descriptive of spiritual wandering. Glancing through the volumes comprising Frost's oeuvre, one finds, then, the pressure of gravity and a real sense that inner weather, poetically speaking, refracts upon, explains, or at least parallels, outer weather. In "The Lesson for Today" the poet explains, "I would have written of me on my stone: / I had a lover's quarrel with the world." To the last, a question of intimacy makes itself evident.

Frost, to recall his pun, was "instinctively Thoreau." He shares the earlier writer's ambiguity, maintaining a commitment, on the one hand, to "being located" (*Walden*) and, on the other, to its ambiguous opposite—what Thoreau called moments of "extra-vagance." One had to know the stones of the place but, Frost knew as well, one had to know when to "put down stones and turn away." The success of poetry, as of love, all depends, really, on how and where you draw the line. In "Walking" Thoreau lets a physical metaphor embody the complexities of an interior journey.

A similar anticipation lingers about Frost's verse, a flickering erotic energy that awakens the hope of intimacy: the verse holds out the promise, as in "The Pasture," of the sharing of secrets and secret places: "You come, too." The verse is a secret preserve, a wild place ordered, closed and protected—into which and through which certain readers receive safe passage. Here the figures of love and poetry meet. Like a relationship between lovers, the poetic text privileges exclusion. Neither offers invitations open to all, since both exclude the "wrong ones." Both assume privilege—private law—although both love and the text exist in publicly formal circumstances. Yet both, in addition, establish domains which are dramatically private. As I have shown, Frost's "The Pasture" demonstrates the tensions between invitation and reserve, the functions of intimacy, that, at the center of Frost's poetic, structure the writing of the verse and control its reading. They promise a sharing of space—a privileged entry into the secrets that the text keeps for itself. A poem, then, quite literally, creates and fences a space. Like a pasture it is half-wild and half-tame, and it represents the difference that human spirit makes in an otherwise natural order.

Berry, like Frost, understood that in love and poetry alike, "making a difference" is the human necessity. "The earth is the genius of our life," he writes, in which a man is "husband, in the oldest sense of the word, having committed himself in multiple marriages to wife, family, farm, community," and finally, to "the cycle of great nature itself."[5] Yet Berry's sense of these engagements is dark: "This steep, half-ruined, lovely place, / this graced and wearing labor / longer than my life, this marriage, / blessed and difficult— / these have a partial radiance that is all my light" (*Clearing* 35). But this, too, recalls Frost in "To Earthward": "Now no joy but lacks salt / That is not dashed with pain / And weariness and fault; / I crave the stain / Of tears, the aftermark / Of almost too much love" (227).

Wendell Berry's *Clearing* is a collection of verse whose subjects, themes, and even title recall Frost's presence, and throughout it reads like a tribute to the older poet. From first to last, then, there seems to be a conscious effort on Berry's part to reverence his roots. Everywhere in his verse one finds the pressure of gravity—the pull of the earth and a commitment to intimacy—that reflects Berry's spiritual lineage. Frost, of course, had shown Berry this necessary union of place and person, and Berry would later expand the conjunction, making it central to his poetics of intimacy. As a final observation, recall how the last poem of Berry's *Clearing* echoes the final poem in Frost's *In the Clearing*. The latter begins,

> In winter in the woods alone
> Against the trees I go.
> I mark a maple for my own
> And lay the maple low.
>
> At four o'clock I shoulder axe
> And in the afterglow
> I link a line of shadowy tracks
> Across the tinted snow.

In "Reverdure" Berry writes, "And so, in the first warmth of the year, / I went up with saw and axe / to cut a way in. I made a road, I made / a thought-way under the trees." Both poets, walking, meditate upon their journeys. Both intimate an end, as Berry says: "an end to words / for a while—for this time, / or for all time. Any end may last" (*Clearing* 52). There may be other clearings yet to make, both poets hint, but knowing

where the limit is, is human, and is enough. For now, both poets con-
clude, in this "country of marriage," it is enough to be "overtired / Of the
great harvest I myself desired" (*Poetry* 69).

NOTES

[1] *Robert Frost: Modern Poetics and the Landscapes of Self* (Durham: Duke UP, 1975) 4.

[2] Wendell Berry, "Elerby," *Collected Poems, 1957-1982* (San Francisco: North Point,
1985) 286. All other citations of Berry's poetry are from this edition and will be
cited in the text.

[3] Hyde Cox and Edward Connery Lathem, eds., *Selected Prose of Robert Frost* (New York:
Holt, Rinehart, and Winston, 1966) 18.

[4] Robert Frost, "The Pasture," in *The Poetry of Robert Frost*, Edward Connery Lathem,
ed. (New York: Henry Holt, 1969) 1. All other citations of Frost's poetry are from
this edition.

[5] *A Place on Earth*, rev. ed. (San Francisco: North Point Press, 1985) 554.

James Wright and Robert Frost: Debts and Diversions

Peter Stitt

Robert Frost was clearly a very important poet to James Wright, a fact that Wright acknowledged on several occasions. When his first book, *The Green Wall*, was chosen by W. H. Auden as the 1957 publication in the Yale Series of Younger Poets, Wright said for quotation on the dust jacket: "I've tried very hard to write in the mode of Robert Frost and Edwin Arlington Robinson. I've wanted to make the poems say something humanly important instead of just showing off with language." The import of this statement is clear enough; Wright is identifying himself with traditionalist American poets rather than with the modernists or postmodernists. That commitment was to last for the duration of his career, though certainly some of the ways in which he used imagery in *Shall We Gather at the River* (1968) and after would have been greatly surprising to Frost and Robinson. I cannot, however, think that Frost would have been much surprised by the quasi-surrealistic nature imagery in *The Branch Will Not Break* (1963).

In 1972, fifteen years after the publication of James Wright's first book, I interviewed him on behalf of *The Paris Review* and asked him what he had learned from Frost. He replied:

> Well, first of all I think there is his profound, terrifying, and very tragic view of the universe, which seems to me true. . . . There is that, but also technically there is something in Frost. He knows how to keep the adjectives out. An example is his poem "Lodged." A very short poem, it has one adverb in it— "actually"—and that one adverb, it seems to me, strikes like a bullet.[1]

While we were talking, Wright quoted the poem, as was his usual practice when discussing poetry. He had an eidetic memory; I once sat in a room with him as he opened a letter from Anthony Hecht containing a new poem, approximately fifty lines in length. He read the poem once and then quoted it to me verbatim, not as a stunt but as the sort of thing he did every day.

"Lodged" is one of Frost's shortest—and least noticed—poems; it appears in *West-Running Brook*, just after "Once by the Pacific":

> The rain to the wind said,
> "You push and I'll pelt."
> They so smote the garden bed
> That the flowers actually knelt,
> And lay lodged—though not dead.
> I know how the flowers felt.[2]

Though Wright presents this poem as an illustration of his point about modifiers, it also bears importantly upon his larger, more philosophical point. But I will save that for later.

The lesson about keeping the adjectives out was an important one for Wright—so important that he seemingly had to keep reminding himself of it throughout his career. As he also explained in our interview, "my chief enemy in poetry is glibness. . . . I speak and write too easily."[3] Generally Wright's glibness shows up through an excessive use of modifiers. A striking example occurs in the fifth section of the first draft of "The Minneapolis Poem"—a section that Wright later entirely deleted from the poem. In the first flush of inspiration, however, he wrote these lines:

> The city fathers have fumigated
> And swept out of sight
> The syphilitic lesbians, hysterical suicides,
> Like bugs down a lye-scarred sewer.
>
> But strange barges
> Drift near the river shore after midnight.
> The insolvent dead row them, calling their mothers.[4]

Though Wright kept the "lye-scarred sewer," the "strange barges," and the "insolvent dead" in the final version of this section, he did change the "hysterical suicides" to "hysterical children" and the "syphilitic lesbians" to "female impersonators," retaining the adjective-noun pattern in both cases. I think it must have been a sense of irritation with his inability to tone this section down that caused Wright simply to delete the whole thing. As an example of non-Frostian glibness, "syphilitic lesbians" is hard to beat.

Before going on to the major point Wright made about his indebtedness to Frost, I want to touch briefly on two other statements he made about the elder poet on the occasion of our interview. At one point, I asked about the strong sense of structure I had found in one of his collections: "Do you in constructing your books generally have that idea of coherence in mind?" Wright answered: "Every time. Did I mention to you Robert Frost's remark—it is a very Horatian remark—that if you

90

have a book of twenty-four poems, the book itself should be the twenty-fifth? And I have tried that every time, every time."[5] I see an interesting distinction here. While Frost wrote many long narrative and dramatic poems, his individual collections are not particularly narrative. What unites the poems in these books is not so much a developing situation we are eager to see solved as a shared attitude toward the world, a unified sensibility. This is probably true as well of Wright's first two books, *The Green Wall* and *Saint Judas* (1959), but beginning with *The Branch Will Not Break* (1963), I think we can see a definite commitment to narrative values in the construction of his collections.[6] So while the commitment to unity is shared by the poets, they tend to diverge in how they achieve it.

The other of Wright's incidental statements on Frost came just after the major statement with which I began this essay. In response to Wright's emphasis on the metaphysical darkness of Frost's poetry, I bemusedly characterized Frost as "America's great nature poet" and asked Wright: "Would you call yourself a nature poet?" He replied: "In part, yes." Rather than being a minor statement, however, this comment might actually provide a key to understanding Wright's major point of comparison between himself and Robert Frost. I think it is safe to say that James Wright is generally recognized as the major American nature poet of his generation, and in this respect he would be the natural heir to Frost. The differences in the ways in which the two deal with nature, however, are more profound than the similarities. For purposes of this discussion, I would like to posit three realms that relate in different ways to one another in the work of these two poets. In the middle I place the realm of nature, meaning not just nature unmediated, the pure nature of the wilderness, but also pastoral nature, the more or less domesticated nature that we find on farms and in parks and poems. On one side of this realm stands the kingdom of God, the metaphysical realm, a possible paradise. On the other side stands the realm of humankind, the world of society as exemplified by the factory and the city, the murderer, the pimp, the police, the prostitute, and the ravages of technology. If this description makes anyone squirm, it must be because this realm scarcely appears in the work of Robert Frost.

Frost writes mostly about the pastoral realm of nature, and he treats it generally in the context of, or in contrast to, the metaphysical realm. But again a distinction is in order; for Frost, paradise — such paradise as there may be for humankind — does not exist beyond nature in the kingdom of God, but within nature, on the farms and in the woods nearby. Indeed, the metaphysical realm is for Frost an object of deep suspicion; it represents not salvation but annihilation. Which is why we must not venture

91

too far from that farm, too far into those woods, for as nature becomes increasingly less domesticated, increasingly more wild, in the poetry of Robert Frost, it seems to approach closer and closer to this dangerous metaphysical realm. Similarly, Frost's relations with God are marked by a deep uncertainty; Frost is profoundly suspicious of God's motives toward humankind. Thus Wright's notion of Frost's "profound, terrifying, and very tragic view of the universe" is based neither upon Frost's treatment of social relations among human beings nor upon his treatment of the relationship that exists between the human realm and the realm of pastoral nature. Rather, Wright's view is based on Frost's sense of the relationship between the human realm and the metaphysical realm. In Frost's poetry, the place where these two realms meet is in the wilderness, and generally speaking, the way God is presented in the poems is through the personification of various aspects of the wilderness.

Which of course is what we see happening in "Lodged," where Frost may be said to present God through his personification of the wind and the rain, which are so concerned to impose subjection first upon the flowers and then, through the agency of the speaker, upon humankind. A more theologically obvious example of this sort of thing occurs in the sonnet "Design," one of Frost's best known and most frightening poems. Here the speaker speculates on the perfectly predatory design inherent in the web built by a white spider upon a flower mutated from blue to white. What can be the purpose of this unnatural conjuction of white-nesses, Frost asks at the end, "but design of darkness to appall?— / If design govern in a thing so small."[7] He almost lets us off the hook with the use of the word *darkness*, his use of the question mark, and his use of the word *If*. Almost, but not quite. Frost does not distinguish generally in his poetry between metaphysical realms of darkness and light; for him, it is all one thing, more dark than light. Elsewhere he is even more explicit in identifying God alone as the author of such appalling designs—for example, in the sonnet "Once by the Pacific," in which a powerful storm approaches not a garden but the California coast. The speaker imagines a huge face in the clouds, as "Great waves looked over others coming in, / And thought of doing something to the shore / That water never did to land before." This will be "a night of dark intent / . . . and not only a night, an age. / Someone had better be prepared for rage. / There would be more than ocean-water broken / Before God's last *Put out the Light* was spoken."[8] Frost gives us no convenient avenue of escape here; his images point directly to the throne of God.

Frost's "profound, terrifying, and very tragic view of the universe," then, exists out at the far end of nature, where that realm merges, through the wilderness, into the realm of a hostile and destructive God. Man belongs on the farm and needs the buffer offered by the wilderness, which isolates him temporarily and imperfectly from the depredations perpetrated by God. Interestingly, given James Wright's acknowledgment of Frost's influence upon him in this area, his own view of the frontier between nature and the metaphysical is entirely different. For him, evil and destructiveness originate in the realm of humankind, the realm of society, rather than in the realm of God. Other "contemporary" poets, however, do have poems in which man is assaulted by abstract forces that seem to originate in the metaphysical realm. John Berryman, for example, has his Dream Song 45, in which Henry is visited first by a series of imposters of a character named, with a capital *R*, Ruin, and then by the real item; Ruin is an ultimate thing in this amusing poem, akin to the destructive God of Frost's poems.[9] And in William Stafford's ironic hunting poem, "Kinds of Winter," the speaker and his companion follow the track of the "big one" into the wilderness, only to discover when they look up that night is falling, and a bad snow storm is overtaking them, covering their own tracks back: "We looked at each other. Our winter had come."[10] Another "big one" had been tracking them.

The lessons in these poems come from beyond the human realm, from the outer reaches of nature or from the realm of God himself. The situation is quite different in the poems of James Wright, where the worst dangers to the protagonist generally come directly from the realm of humankind. We can see this everywhere in Wright's work, not least in "The Minneapolis Poem," to which I have already referred. The good guys in this poem are the homeless and the poor, the winos and the prostitutes, the victims; the bad guys are the police, the adolescent toughs, the wealthy businessmen in their towers and big cars. This is a poem in which "Split-lipped homosexuals limp in terror of assault. / High school backfields search under benches / Near the Post Office. Their faces are the rich / Raw bacon without eyes. / The Walker Art Center crowd stare / At the Guthrie Theater."[11]

And just as he despises the city and its minions, James Wright idealizes nature and the farm. Thus, at the end of this poem his speaker utters this pastoral prayer: "I want to be lifted up / By some great white bird unknown to the police, / And soar for a thousand miles and be carefully hidden / Modest and golden as one last corn grain / Stored with the secrets of the wheat and the mysterious lives / Of the unnamed poor." The pastoral realm is no lasting solution for Wright, as it is for Frost, for even in nature, even on the farm, Wright could find evidence of the befouling influence of humankind, as in the late and ironic poem "Ohioan Pastoral":

> On the other side
> Of Salt Creek, along the road, the barns topple
> And snag among the orange rinds,
> Oil cans, cold balloons of lovers.
> One barn there
> Sags, sags and oozes
> Down one side of the copperous gully.
> The limp whip of a sumac dangles
> Gently against the body of a lost
> Bathtub, while high in the flint-cracks
> And the wild grimed trees, on the hill,
> A buried gas main
> Long ago tore a black gutter into the mines.
> And now it hisses among the green rings
> On fingers in coffins.[12]

One of the major patterns of imagery in the book from which this poem is taken, *The Journey* (published posthumously in 1982), concerns the effects of human pollution not just upon nature but upon cities, artworks, and persons as well.

Indeed, the further one gets from society and the city in Wright's poems, the closer one approaches paradise. Not that Wright concerns himself with the wilderness, which almost never appears in his poems. But the kitchen garden and the cornfield seem always but a step away from the Garden of Eden, where the lion lies down with the lamb. The process of idealization is perhaps most clear in one of Wright's best known poems, "Lying in a Hammock at William Duffy's Farm in Pine Island, Minnesota." The speaker, a refugee from the city, notices first "a bronze butterfly, / . . . / Blowing like a leaf in green shadow," then "cowbells follow[ing] one another / Into the distances of the afternoon," then "The droppings of last year's horses / Blaz[ing] up into golden stones." Within such a perfectly idealized landscape, is it any wonder that this speaker should feel that he has "wasted [his] life" in the city?[13]

That pastoral nature is the gateway to paradise is made explicitly clear in another of Wright's best known poems, "A Blessing," where the speaker and his friend stop their car, walk significantly away from the highway that attaches them to the city, and enter a field occupied by two horses. So transforming is this experience that our speaker concludes: "Suddenly I realize / That if I stepped out of my body I would break / Into blossom."[14] So powerful is Wright's idealization of the natural world

94

that it even allows him to treat death positively in his final work. In the poem "This Journey," for example, death is represented by the figure of a predatory spider who—far from being presented negatively—shines "Slender and fastidious, the golden hair / Of daylight along her shoulders."[15] This spider lives in a landscape of ruin and desolation, surrounded by signs of death and at the mercy of a dust storm. And yet she endures and triumphs, leading Wright to the astonishing and generalized conclusion he gives this poem:

> The secret
> Of this journey is to let the wind
> Blow its dust all over your body,
> To let it go on blowing, to step lightly, lightly
> All the way through your ruins, and not to lose
> Any sleep over the dead, who surely
> Will bury their own, don't worry.

Both Frost and Wright might be said to have had a "profound, terrifying, and very tragic view of the universe," but they are looking in opposite directions. James Wright's tragic gaze is directed at human life lived within society, within the city, where all forms of pollution, both moral and physical, are dominant. He longed for that imperishable realm beyond death and time, the closest analogue of which occurs within the pastoral realm of nature. Frost too idealizes nature, to the extent that he was most at home setting his poems within it. He did not like to deviate much to either side, neither to the cities where large numbers of people come together, nor to the wilderness, where the domination of a harsh and angry God is most evident. Thus Frost feared death, which would commit him to the clutches of this God and deprive him of the natural realm in which he is so comfortable. James Wright, on the other hand, almost welcomed death, so miserable was he in the vale of tears we know as human life. The greatest and most enduring area of agreement between the two poets is in their mutual veneration of nature, the pastoral realm. Where they diverge the most is in their identification of the negative pole, the source of ultimate danger.

NOTES

[1] Peter Stitt, "Interview with James Wright," in his *The World's Hieroglyphic Beauty: Five American Poets* (Athens: U of Georgia P, 1985) 201.

[2] Robert Frost, "Lodged," *Complete Poems of Robert Frost* (New York: Holt, Rinehart and Winston, 1949) 315.

[3] Stitt 206.

[4] Wright's manuscripts are now available to scholars at the University of Minnesota Libraries.

[5] Stitt 205.

[6] For a detailed discussion of the narrative structure of one of Wright's books, see my essay "The Quest Motif in James Wright's *The Branch Will Not Break*," in Dave Smith, ed., *The Pure Clear Word: Essays on the Poetry of James Wright* (Urbana: U of Illinois P, 1982) 65-77.

[7] Frost 396.

[8] Frost 314.

[9] John Berryman, "45," *77 Dream Songs* (New York: Farrar, Straus, 1964) 49.

[10] William Stafford, "Kinds of Winter," in his *Writing the Australian Crawl: Views on the Writer's Vocation* (Ann Arbor: U of Michigan P, 1978) 74.

[11] James Wright, "The Minneapolis Poem," *Above the River: The Complete Poems* (New York: Farrar, Straus and Giroux, 1990) 147-49.

[12] Wright 348.

[13] Wright 122.

[14] Wright 143.

[15] Wright 338.

"For Robert Frost":
Form and Content in the Poetry of Galway Kinnell

Nancy L. Tuten

In his 1939 essay, "The Figure a Poem Makes," Robert Frost wrote what has come to be one of his best-known statements about the nature of poetry:

> It begins in delight and ends in wisdom. . . . No one can really hold that the ecstasy should be static and stand still in one place. It begins in delight, it inclines to the impulse, it assumes direction with the first line laid down, it runs a course of lucky events, and ends in a clarification of life—not necessarily a great clarification, such as sects and cults are founded on, but a momentary stay against confusion. (18)

Twenty-two years later, accused of writing poetry that seemed more tentative than affirmative, Galway Kinnell seemed to echo Frost with his response:

> It would be nice if in a single poem one could resolve a given problem forever—come to terms with it once and for all. But each poem comes out of its own moment. (*Walking* 28)

In order to establish their new brand of modernism, Kinnell and his contemporaries felt the need to move away from the formalism espoused by Eliot, Pound, and Frost in particular (Guimond 18). Nonetheless, as revealed in his poem, "For Robert Frost," Kinnell is acutely aware of the concerns that are most central to Frost's work. His tone is one of respect, for even though the two poets embrace conflicting views about the manner in which poetry should be written, Kinnell recognizes that they are merely using different methods to probe similar questions and combat the same fears.

While form may be the foremost difference between the modernists and their successors, the latter were more specifically concerned with the overuse of rhyme and meter to the exclusion of content. When, in a 1976 interview, Margaret Edwards accused Kinnell of "thinking that form is itself an evasion," the poet zeroed in on the real problem:

I don't think the term "form" should be applied only to such things as stanzas of uniform size, rhyme schemes, metrical patterns, and so on—elements which may be regarded as external trappings.... Form properly speaking also has to do with the inner shape of the poem. Some of the most "formal" poems are rather formless in this sense: they change subject, lose the thread of their arguments, and lack the sense of suspense and sense of culmination that come from the pursuit of one goal. (*Walking* 105)

Kinnell dislikes poetry that has become little more than a structural word game: "I don't think it's the formal qualities in themselves that make one feel a poem is just a *tour de force*. It's when the poem is at the mercy of the form" (*Walking* 95). Kinnell feels that "for the modern poet rhyme and meter, having lost their sacred meaning and natural basis, amount to little more than mechanical aids for writing," because "rhymes in [the Elizabethans'] poems are a way of acknowledging the everlasting return of things" in which we no longer believe (*Walking* 29). Frost, however, rather than allowing his verse to be at the mercy of form, uses rhyme and meter to create order in a world lacking in sureties. In "For Robert Frost," Kinnell expresses a clear understanding of—and even a respect for— what language and form meant to the elder poet.

The poem opens with a question: "Why do you talk so much / Robert Frost?" (*Avenue* 142). Having spent the day visiting the poet at his farm in Ripton, Kinnell says he "drove off at dusk / worn out and aching / In both ears" but "never got the chance / To put the question." While at first the "question" seems almost flippant, the tone shifts abruptly a few lines later with the somber suggestion that perhaps for Frost talk is "distracting from something worse." Indeed, in a number of Frost's poems, conversation emerges as one way of maintaining order in the face of confusion. "Home Burial" clearly expresses his awareness of the destruction that can result when communication breaks down. When the husband says, "Three foggy mornings and one rainy day / Will rot the best birch fence a man can build," he is expressing his newly-experienced understanding of the individual's ineffectuality (*Poetry* 54). But his wife hears only the literal words and believes that because he can talk about commonplace events, he could not possibly be experiencing the grief that consumes her. While he desperately pleads with her to talk to him, to share her grief in order to find consolation, she refuses to mention the death of their child or to allow him to speak of it in her presence. The title is appropriate since their failure to communicate leads to the "death" of both their marriage and their home.

Clearly, Frost believes that the individual's best defense against the confusion of the universe is the ability to combat it through the use of language. Stronger still is that power when words conform to rhyme and meter. We think, of course, of "Stopping by Woods on a Snowy Evening," wherein each stanza's rhyme scheme is governed by the last word in the third line of the previous verse. This control reflects the speaker's struggle throughout the poem to overcome the temptation to plunge into the woods. James M. Cox calls the poem "the counter-spell against the invitation, the act by which the traveler regains dominion of his will" (151). When in the final stanza he decides to remain in the clearing and resist the call to abandon order, Frost reinforces his decision by having all four lines rhyme and by repeating the last phrase twice.

Kinnell believes that while it is often difficult to make rhymed verse sound "reasonably natural and idiomatic," the limitation of this form can in one way make it easier to write:

> . . . there are many words in English for which there are only one or two rhymes, and many with no rhymes at all. . . . The poem has to confine itself to meanings that one of the available rhyme words can accommodate. It's here that rhyming poetry is "easier" than free verse. Seeing the possible rhyme words taking shape out there ahead of you, you aim for them. So the rhymes lead you forward and actively aid the composition of the poem.   (*Walking* 94)

Yet, on another occasion, and in defense of his own preference for free verse, Kinnell argues that rhyme and meter force the poet to "say something, perhaps anything, which fulfills the formal requirements." He adds, "If you were walking through snow, rhyming would be like following a set of footprints continually appearing ahead of you" (Guimond 39). What does appeal to Kinnell is the idea of being pulled forward by the predetermined rhyme scheme in order to discover the meaning of the poem; on one occasion he states, "In his best poems, Frost comes out with mysterious utterances that surprise even him. There is a lot of control and deliberate technique in most of his poems, but this doesn't stop him from making sudden frightening probes into the unsayable" (*Walking* 65). In part three of "For Robert Frost," Kinnell pays homage to Frost's adherence to form by figuratively "following the footsteps" of the elder poet: "Once, walking in winter in Vermont, / In the snow, I followed a set of footprints / That aimed for the woods" (*Avenue* 143). Metaphorically, Kinnell places himself in Frost's shoes and can, therefore, infuse his poem with lines from works that embody the most central of Frost's concerns.

Before Kinnell embarks on this poetic journey through Frost's major themes, however, he establishes in part two of the poem that all of Frost's poetry springs from the heart of his being. The final stanza of "Reluctance" expresses the idea which is at the core of Frost's best work: the belief that even when the body can no longer function to maintain control, the heart does not abandon the struggle. Frost writes,

> Ah, when to the heart of man
>   Was it ever less than a treason
> To go with the drift of things,
>   To yield with a grace to reason,
> And bow and accept the end
>   Of a love or a season? (*Poetry* 30)

In Kinnell's poem, Frost stands "lonely before millions," about to give a reading at the presidential inauguration, but the sunlight is too bright and his "eyes / Wrecked from writing poems / For us" cannot see the printed words. Even the "managers of the event / said, Boys this is it, / The sonofabitch poet / Is gonna croak." It seems as if the aged poet will be unable to summon the power of language, but the point in Frost's "Reluctance" is that the heart endures beyond physical limitations; Frost puts aside his paper and draws forth from his "great faithful heart / The poem" (*Avenue* 143).

In the third section of "For Robert Frost" Kinnell uses quotations and paraphrases from works of Frost in which he portrays the speaker—usually himself—as yearning for solitude away from human interaction. Kinnell carefully alludes to those poems which find Frost "on the borderline between the open fields and the winter woods, nature and society, life and death" (Guimond 41). The footprints Kinnell follows are "aimed for the woods." As Donald J. Greiner points out, "the meaning of the woods is never constant" in Frost's work (382), but most critics agree that the woods represent an invitation to the poet-figure "which invites him to forsake his daily business" (384). In an effort to experience most fully the fear and loneliness expressed in so much of Frost's work, Kinnell creates this imaginary figure of Frost, "An old creature in a huge, clumsy overcoat, / Lifting his great boots through the drifts" (*Avenue* 143-44) and follows him on his journey.

James P. Dougherty explains that in most of his poetry Frost "represents himself in a momentary equipoise between the desire to plunge into the darkness of the forest, and a restraining mixture of fear and commitment to 'promises' in the world of men" (208). Kinnell chooses, instead, to follow his imaginary Frost "far in the pillared dark" (*Avenue* 143), for this journey, like the one in Frost's "Directive," requires the traveler to take more risks, to follow a guide "Who only has at heart your getting lost" (*Poetry* 377). At this point in "For Robert Frost," Kinnell quotes the phrase "those dark trees" from "Into My Own," the first poem in Frost's first book, a poem which finds the isolated poet diving into the lovely, dark, and deep woods of his inner self. Kinnell would find more meaning in this kind of risk than in the balance maintained in a poem like "Stopping by Woods." In one essay he writes,

> If we are willing to face the worst in ourselves, we also have to accept the risk . . . that probing into one's own wretchedness one may just dig up more wretchedness. What justifies the risk is the hope that in the end the search may open and transfigure us. ("Poetry" 67)

Both Kinnell and Frost realize that in order to define what is meaningful, or, as Frost says in "Directive," in order to get to the source of existence, one must travel beyond all that is familiar and venture "into the pathless wood" (*Avenue* 144). Kinnell uses a quotation from "Acquainted With the Night" to emphasize the poet-figure's need to escape all human inter-action on this journey of self-discovery: "He had outwalked the farthest city light" and is now standing at the edge of the abyss, the "white, uncertain — / The night too dark to know" (*Poetry* 255). Having followed his Frost-figure to this place of "dark trees, for which no saying is dark enough," Kinnell reaches the climax of "For Robert Frost" at the end of this third section. Section four begins with two simple but crucial words: "He turned." Kinnell's point is that for Frost, as well as for himself, the journey is successful only if it enables him to turn back to life in the world: "*Love, / Love of things, duty,* he said, / And made his way back . . .*" (*Avenue* 144). Regardless of what the woods might mean in a particular Frost poem, they must never represent an escape from responsibility. As Greiner aptly states, the woods can afford only an opportunity for retreat when "necessary to compose the self before returning to humanity" (385).

Kinnell is very much aware of the temptation to plunge into the "woods" and not return. He explains death as having two aspects, "the extinction, which we fear, and the flowing away into the universe, which we desire" (*Walking* 23), but the overriding statement in Kinnell's work is that which is expressed in his 1980 collection, *Mortal Acts, Mortal Words*: by accepting both the mundane acts of everyday life and mortality itself, the individual can find a form of grace, a transcendence that paradox-ically must not seek to rise above the earthly body but rather is found within the physical. Frost expresses the same idea in "Birches" when he says "Earth's the right place for love" (*Poetry* 122) or in "To Earthward" where the persona learns that only through love of the world can he come to discover the love of another person. In the second half of this poem, the speaker comes to love imperfection; one needs to feel roughness and to know sadness, for these provide the raw material out of which form is created. For both Kinnell and Frost, the experience in the woods must culminate in the creation of some kind of order that enables life to be lived more fully.

When in section four of "For Robert Frost" Kinnell says that the poet "made his way back to the shelter / No longer sheltering him, the house / Where everything was turning to words" (*Avenue* 144), he once again stresses Frost's need for form to protect him from nonhuman otherness. The second stanza of part four alludes to Frost's "West-Running Brook," a poem about the human need to put up some kind of resistance to the "universal cataract of death / That spends to nothingness—" (*Poetry* 259). Kinnell says that Frost would "think on the white wave, / Folded back, that rides in place on the obscure / Pouring of this life to the sea—" (*Avenue* 144), an overt references to the wave in "West-Running Brook" that is "Flung backward on itself in one white wave" that "runs counter to itself" (*Poetry* 258). The poem demands a backward journey against the current towards the source of existence "long before we were from any creature" (*Poetry* 259), or, in Kinnell's words, toward the "nonhuman, . . . the basic context of human existence." He explains that "when in the presence of wind, or the night sky, or the sea, or less spectacular instances of the nonhuman . . . we are reminded both of the kinship and the separation between ourselves and what is beyond us" (*Walking* 88). Frost would add, "and what was before us," but the point would be the same; just as the journey into the dark woods involves a risk, the need for form to order life requires a confrontation with the nonhuman otherness that threatens to annihilate us.

The danger of the journey is once more alluded to in the final section of the poem when Kinnell refers to Frost as a man "whose calling / Was to set up in the wilderness of his country, / At whatever cost, a man who would be his own man" (*Avenue* 145). As it is in "Directive," this emphasis on finding the spiritual by delving into the material is the major theme in one of Frost's last poems, "Kitty Hawk." The flight of the Wright Brothers was risky. But Frost asserts, just as God "risked" spirit in substantiation, the individual must be concerned with achieving transcendence through the physical. The quest in "Directive" is for wholeness, to "drink and be whole again beyond confusion" (*Poetry* 379). In "Kitty Hawk," the "holiness of wholeness" is expressed in the idea that "We may get control / If not of the whole, / Of at least some part / Where not too immense, / So by craft or art / We can give the part / Wholeness in a sense" (*Poetry* 440-41).

In the final lines of "For Robert Frost," when Kinnell refers to Frost's "calling," he alludes to the last stanza of the poem "Two Tramps in Mud Time," where the speaker tells us that his "object in living is to unite / [his] avocation and [his] vocation" (*Poetry* 277). "Where love and need are one," chopping wood is more than just a chore to be accomplished; it is one way that he exerts control over nonhuman otherness. Similarly, in "The Woodpile," the person who cuts the cord of maple wood is "Someone who lived in turning to fresh tasks," someone who values the act of chopping above any potential usefulness the wood might have (*Poetry* 101). Kinnell would readily identify with this idea in Frost because time and again his own work emphasizes the necessity of the struggle encountered in the everyday trials by existence. "Hard work concedes the reality of this world," he stated in a 1976 interview. For both poets, the intensity with which one approaches an ordinary act determines the level to which he or she gains insight into mortality and, thus, establishes control over confusion.

When, in "For Robert Frost," Kinnell says that Frost "dwelt in access to that which other men / Have burnt all their lives to get near," he refers to the elder poet's ability to order life temporarily through his poetry. He only dwells in access to the source, however, for Frost realizes that one cannot sustain control. The poet must continue to write poems in order to maintain the balance in life that the form provides. While Kinnell chooses not to employ strict rhyme and meter in his verse, he nonetheless recognizes the value of language as a means for dealing with life. In his words,

> Everyone knows that human existence is incomplete. . . . Writing is a way of trying to understand the incompleteness and, if not to heal it, at least to get beyond whatever is merely baffling and oppressive about it. (*Walking* 105)

Kinnell believes that each poem should come out of its own moment. Like Frost, he uses his art to run a course of events that he hopes will end in a clarification of life — in Frost's words, not necessarily a great one, but a "momentary stay against confusion."

WORKS CITED

Cox, James M. "Robert Frost and the Edge of the Clearing." *The Virginia Quarterly Review* 35 (Winter 1959) 51-55.

Dougherty, James P. "Robert Frost's 'Directive' to the Wilderness." *American Quarterly* 18 (1966) 208-19.

Frost, Robert. "The Figure a Poem Makes." *Selected Prose*. Ed. Hyde Cox and Edward Connery Lathem. New York: Holt, Rinehart and Winston, 1966.

———. *The Poetry of Robert Frost*. Ed. Edward Connery Lathem. New York: Holt, Rinehart and Winston, 1969.

Greiner, Donald J. "Robert Frost's Dark Woods and the Function of Metaphor." *Frost: Centennial Essays I*. Ed. Jac Tharpe. Jackson: U of Mississippi P, 1976. 373-88.

Guimond, James. *Seeing and Healing: A Study of the Poetry of Galway Kinnell*. Port Washington, NY: Associated Faculty P, 1984.

Kinnell, Galway. *The Avenue Bearing the Initial of Christ into the New World: Poems 1946-1964*. Boston: Houghton Mifflin, 1974.

———. *Mortal Acts, Mortal Words*. Boston: Houghton Mifflin, 1980.

———. "Poetry, Personality, and Death." *Field* 4 (1971) 56-77.

———. *Walking Down the Stairs: Selections from Interviews*. Ann Arbor: U of Michigan P, 1978.

CONTRIBUTORS

JONATHAN N. BARRON is Assistant Professor of English at the University of North Carolina at Charlotte. He has written on Wordsworth and on Jewish-American poetry, and is currently at work on *What Happened to Poetry?*, a book about contemporary American poetry.

RICHARD J. CALHOUN is Alumni Distinguished Professor of English at Clemson University, where he is Executive Editor of *The South Carolina Review*. He has served as president of the Robert Frost Society and is currently working on a book on Frost and the sonnet.

PAMELA DAVIS teaches at the Brentwood School in Los Angeles. Her essay was first read at the Modern Language Association Convention in New York, 1992.

DONALD J. GREINER, Carolina Professor of English at the University of South Carolina, is the author of *Robert Frost: The Poet and His Critics*. He has published several books on twentieth-century American literature; his latest is *Woman without Men: Female Bonding and the American Novel of the 1980s*.

DOROTHY JUDD HALL, author of *Robert Frost: Contours of Belief*, teaches in the Religion Department of Boston University. A Visiting Scholar to the Jesuit Institute in 1993 at Boston College, she has published widely on Frost.

EDWARD INGEBRETSEN, S.J. is an Assistant Professor of English at Georgetown University. Among his publications are studies on Frost, the American Gothic, and American Christianity. He is the author of the forthcoming book, *Maps of Heaven, Maps of Hell: Religious Terror as Memory in American Fantasy*.

MORDECAI MARCUS, Professor of English at the University of Nebraska-Lincoln, holds degrees from Brooklyn College, New York University, and the University of Kansas. He taught at Rutgers, Kansas, and Purdue before coming to Nebraska. He is the author of *The Poems of Robert Frost: An Explication*, plus many critical essays and six chapbooks of poems.

PETER J. STANLIS is the author of eleven books and over 100 articles and reviews on legal, political, educational, and literary subjects. He was a co-founder of the American Society for Eighteenth-Century Studies and a personal friend of Robert Frost from 1939 to the poet's death in 1963.

PETER STITT, Editor of *The Gettysburg Review*, is Professor of English at Gettysburg College. He is currently completing a book on contemporary American poetry and is at work on the authorized biography of poet James Wright. In 1993, Stitt was the first recipient of the PEN/Nora Magid Award for Excellence in Editing.

NANCY L. TUTEN, Associate Professor of English at Columbia College (SC), is currently editing a collection of critical essays on Galway Kinnell. While most of her scholarship has centered on Kinnell's poetry, her work also includes studies of Whitman, Roethke, and Alice Walker.

EARL J. WILCOX is editor of *The Robert Frost Review* and Director of the Robert Frost Society. Since 1980 he has arranged more than a dozen sessions on Frost for regional and national conferences. In addition to books on Frost, he has also published extensively on Jack London. In 1994 he will become Executive Director of the College English Association.

1975   1   *Samuel Johnson's Library: An Annotated Guide*, Donald Greene

        2   *The Sale Catalogue of Samuel Johnson's Library: A Facsimile Edition*, J. D. Fleeman

        3   *Swift's Vision of Evil: A Comparative Study of "A Tale of a Tub" and "Gulliver's Travels,"* Volume I, *A Tale of a Tub*, Philip Pinkus

        4   *Swift's Vision of Evil*, Volume II, *Gulliver's Travels*, Philip Pinkus

1976   5   *Dryden and Future Shock*, William Frost

        6   *Henry Fielding's "Tom Jones" and the Romance Tradition*, Henry K. Miller.

        7   *The Achievement of Thomas More*, Richard J. Schoeck

1977   8   *The Postromantic Consciousness of Ezra Pound*, George Bornstein

        9   *Eighteenth-Century Arguments for Immortality and Johnson's "Rasselas,"* R. G. Walker

     10   *E. M. Forster's Posthumous Fiction*, Norman Page

1978 11   *Paradise in the Age of Milton*, U. Milo Kaufmann

     12   *The Slandered Woman in Shakespeare*, Joyce H. Sexton

     13   *Jane Austen on Love*, Juliet McMaster

     14   *C. S. Lewis's "Great War" with Owen Barfield*, Lionel Adey

1979 15   *The Arnoldian Principle of Flexibility*, William Robbins

     16   *Frankenstein's Creation: The Book, The Monster, and Human Reality*, David Ketterer

     17   *Christopher Smart's Verse Translation of Horace's "Odes,"* Arthur Sherbo, ed.

     18   *Gertrude Stein: Autobiography and the Problem of Narration*, Shirley Neuman

1980 19   *Daniel Defoe's Moral and Rhetorical Ideas*, Robert James Merrett

     20   *Studies in Robertson Davies' Deptford Trilogy*, R. G. Lawrence and S. L. Macey, eds.

     21   *Pater and His Early Critics*, Franklin E. Court

1981 22   *The Curve of Return: D. H. Lawrence's Travel Books*, Del Ivan Janik

     23   *The Educational World of Daniel Defoe*, Donald P. Leinster-Mackay

     24   *The Libraries of George Eliot and George Henry Lewes*, William Baker

1982 25   *John Ruskin and Alfred Hunt: New Letters and the Record of a Friendship*, R. Secor

     26   *The Cover of the Mask: The Autobiographers in Charlotte Brontë's Fiction*, A. Tromley

     27   *Charles Olson and Edward Dahlberg: A Portrait of a Friendship*, John Cech

1983 28   *The Road From Horton: Looking Backwards in "Lycidas,"* J. Martin Evans

     29   *Dryden's Dualities*, Ruth Salvaggio

     30   *The Return of the Good Soldier: Ford Madox Ford and Violet Hunt's 1917 Diary*, Robert Secor and Marie Secor

1984 31   *The Splintering Frame: The Later Fiction of H. G. Wells*, William J. Scheick

     32   *The Dynamic Self: Browning's Poetry of Duration*, Samuel L. Chell

     33   *George Moore's Correspondence with the Mysterious Countess*, David B. Eakin and Robert Langenfeld, eds.